Praise for A Drop in The Ocean

A Drop in the Ocean is a book for anyone curious to read an honest account of how challenging, inspiring, and ultimately rewarding it can be to venture across the open water with only your vessel, experience, and wits to guide you. Along with describing the realities of exhaustion, seasickness, and bruises, Jasna also interweaves moments of magic and this why her book is so important. *A Drop in the Ocean* doesn't romanticize an ocean crossing but shows both its difficulty and also its enchantment. These are the pleasures of ocean sailing that can only be experienced firsthand or read about in books like Jasna's. The beauty of the ocean is not just found when the wind and waves are perfect and in the right direction, but in what the sea forces you to do when they are not. Jasna's personal realizations and her final sense of achievement are a straightforward, honest, and accurate portrayal of a first time ocean voyage.

There are still places in the world that many people will never visit, like the famed islands of the South Pacific and luckily there are also still people in the world adventurous enough to travel across an ocean by sailboat to experience them firsthand and share those stories with us.

Charlotte Kaufman
Author, sailor and founder of Women Who Sail

Also by Jasna Tuta

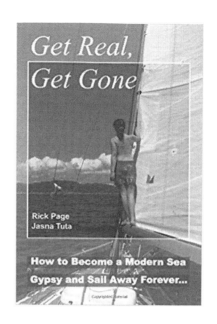

Get Real, Get Gone: How to Become a Modern Sea Gypsy and Sail Away Forever by Rick Page and Jasna Tuta

PRAISE FOR

GET REAL, GET GONE

"Don't even think of buying a boat until you have read this book."

Tom Cunliffe, legendary sailor and author of *The Complete Ocean Skipper*

"More than a how-to manual for the would-be world traveler, *Get Real, Get Gone* also tells how to live life to the fullest and make every day an adventure. You'll learn a lot, and laugh a lot, reading this book."

Marjorie Preston, *Good Old Boat Magazine*

A Drop in The Ocean

Copyright © 2018 Jasna Tuta.

Tuta, Jasna

A Drop in The Ocean

Editing: Rick Page

Photography: Jasna Tuta and Rick Page

Proofreading: Judy Mangle

Front cover design: Tanja Tuta

First edition, November 2018

ISBN 9781728946894 (paperback)

Self-published by Jasna Tuta

www.jasnatuta.com

A Drop in The Ocean

By

Jasna Tuta

This book is dedicated to Rick, who made all of this possible.

He is the best captain I could wish for. He knows how to calm me down in the middle of an emergency and how to make me laugh when the skies are gray. He really is the sun in my sky.

Contents

Preface

Crossing an ocean in a little sailboat is always a big deal, no matter how many times you may have done it before. But the very first time is also the most unforgettable, infused as it is with anticipation of the totally unknown.

If you had told me twelve years ago that one day I would cross the biggest ocean of all in a tiny sailboat with my English boyfriend, I would have laughed. I was just out of university and excited about embarking upon my quest to become the world's best schoolteacher.

So how did I get from a Slovenian primary school to an uninhabited Polynesian atoll?

I could say that it all started with a sabbatical year dedicated to travel, but the truth is that my life changed the day I met a small, blond Englishman at a music concert deep in rural Australia.

Not only did I find a special person I had an instant connection with, but Rick later helped me discover a world I was not even aware existed: the world of the liveaboard sailor.

The sea has always been a big part of my life. I spent many years sailing with friends on various boats in local regattas and worked as a sailing coach for children on dinghies, but I knew nothing of sailing as a lifestyle choice. It certainly never occurred to me that someone could live in a boat instead of a house. I remember once hearing a rumor of a sailor in Trieste who had his boat listed as his main residence in all his documents. My reaction was incredulous.

"What a nut job!" I exclaimed.

That less than charitable reaction makes me laugh today as I imagine people saying the same about me. (To be honest, I rather like it - I am secretly proud of my madness.)

I still remember how happy I felt the first time I held in my hand a document giving my address as:

'Jasna Tuta, living on a boat in the bay of La Paz, Mexico.'

Almost nine years have passed since I moved aboard a sailboat. I call my former existence (when I lived in a flat, paid bills, drove a car, and went to work) 'my previous life,' because it really seems a lifetime away.

Today I look back at the decision to travel the world as one of my smarter moves (although there is not much competition for this accolade), but I remember well the fear of leaving the known quantities of job, apartment, family, friends, and jumping into the unknown.

Of course, such decisions are never easy. We always prefer to stick with the known, because we feel safe and like to believe that a familiar environment helps us predict the future.

But one day I finally accepted that I wasn't happy and that I never would be if I continued to ignore my extremely itchy feet. So, gathering my courage, I bought a one-way ticket to the other side of the world.

Embarking on such a trip, one can be sure of only two things. The first is that one's life will change in some way.

The second is that it will be almost impossible to predict the nature of that change.

My own journey took me to a sailing boat where I found love and happiness. Now everything I have is here on my floating twenty-square meters. I live here, I eat here, and I sleep here. I even work here. The boat gives me everything: shelter, recreation, a sense of purpose, and a chance to earn a small wage by writing about my adventures.

Over the years, I have written literally hundreds of articles about my new lifestyle and have been pleasantly surprised by the amount of interest and positive feedback that it has been my good fortune to receive. People from all walks of life have contacted me asking how we do various everyday things, such as washing or cooking or finding our way. So, several years later on a long overdue visit home, I decided to go on a mini-tour around the libraries, sailing clubs, and local schools of Slovenia and Italy to present details of my new liveaboard lifestyle and hopefully answer the many questions I am most often asked by my fellow countrymen. Packing a little projector and some photos in the back of a small, borrowed car, I set out in the snows of a European winter to paint a picture of tropical paradise in cold, draughty halls to people dreaming of sunshine whilst bundled up in coats and scarves.

As you may predict, many of the questions I was asked on this series of talks were of a fairly similar nature to the ones I received via email and I had developed at least a little skill in answering them. One thing that did catch me out, though, was a particular question to which I had no real answer:

"How does it feel to cross an ocean on a sailboat for the very first time?"

This was not a question that I had really prepared for and I found it next to impossible to give a considered reply. The first few times it came up, I gave some glib answer and quickly moved on. Yet at each new venue, this thorny question would pop up again until eventually I was forced to give it some actual thought and found that the answer was surprisingly complicated.

Hence this book.

In the following pages, I have tried to answer this question as honestly as I can. I have no interest in embellishment, the fictionalizing of events, or hyperbole. My purpose is to paint a fair picture and a realistic narrative that will satisfy those who seek the reality from the fiction.

To accomplish this, I have had to cover the many different facets and contradictions that comprise life at sea. The result is a mixture of events, thoughts, memories, and feelings. Some are exciting, some important, some funny, and some meaningless. All of them are true.

So, if you have ever wondered what it is genuinely like to tremble on the edge of a vast ocean, to raise the sails and head into the unknown, to journey from the desperate lows of fear and tears to the joyous highs of laughter and accomplishment, then step aboard. You are most welcome.

Introduction

I didn't fully realize what I had got myself into until I was standing in a busy foreign street, as far away from my hometown as it is possible to be, amongst people I did not know, all jabbering away in a language I did not understand.

I had made it to Australia. But now what?

This was my first long-haul trip. I had been dreaming about it for years, but now the reality had kicked in and I was getting a little concerned. Where was I going to live? How hard was it going to be to learn English? Would I find a job? How long before I would run out of savings and end up living under a bridge? A million questions joined hands in the quest to make me nervous.

I started my Aussie odyssey by volunteering on an organic farm in the Glasshouse Mountains near Brisbane, where I would spend each morning picking organic vegetables under the burning Australian sun. In the afternoons, I would jump on my bicycle and ride to the next town for English lessons. I was extremely lucky to find an extraordinary English teacher on maternity leave just minutes from the farm. Thanks to her diligent attention, I quickly had enough of the basics to get by without sounding too much like the less decipherable one of the Super Mario Brothers. As December approached, though, I began to feel a little homesick. I would imagine myself all alone on Christmas Eve while my family in Italy would be having our traditional noisy dinner and mountain of gifts.

I was saved from my reverie by Katherine, an Aussie country girl who worked on the farm with me. She saw that I was a little down in the mouth and handed me a lifeline:

"Let's spend the Christmas holiday at Woodford."

"What is Woudfurt?" I asked in my fledgling English.

"It's a music festival. It's amazing. It's huge!" she said, handing me the booklet she had grabbed from her car.

I scrolled through the pages: African dancers, art workshops, theater plays, circus acrobats, and fabulous musicians from all over the world. It certainly looked like something that could help fill the empty space normally occupied by my mum's Christmas dinner. Conveniently, the whole festival started on Christmas Eve and ended on January the second, making it a perfect distraction for the terminally homesick.

The only problem was, at $500 a ticket, it was quite a stretch for our rather meager budgets, so we decided to apply as volunteers which would give us free entry in return for helping with the smooth running of the event. Our applications were successful, and I was lucky to land the rather interesting (and slightly cushy) job of making coffee for the performers. This was a great way to start practicing my English and a welcome change from being half-baked to death scrabbling around in the dirt picking strawberries under the unforgiving Aussie sun.

The Woodford Festival is indeed an astonishing event, way above the standard you would expect in this far-flung corner of the world. Amazing musicians and performers from all corners of the globe and the only thing they have in common being excellence. The acts range from flamenco, to opera, to reggae, to blues and soul. Jazz and Cuban music compete with a spectacular array of physical performers in a seven-day assault on the senses. Oh, and the food is fantastic too. Perfect.

In one of the many workshops was a man who made paper lanterns and butterflies. Everybody who poked their head inside his colorful canvas cavern was encouraged to write their wishes for the following year on a paper butterfly and pop it into one of the many lanterns he had made. These would then be released into the sky on New Year's Eve and burst into flames some miles into the air. This would (apparently) ensure the enclosed wishes would come true by causing a major forest fire somewhere in Queensland. Encouraged by this, I took a little purple butterfly and confessed my wishes to it in silver ink.

Before I left Italy, it is fair to say that my love life had been less than stellar. I had made some spectacularly bad choices, the most recent being an unrequited pursuit that had drained all my energy and robbed me of a great deal of joy. With the help of a good friend, I sat down to write a list of the qualities my next romantic partner would exemplify so I could recognize him were I lucky enough to cross his path. Because those qualities were all really about positive energy in one form or another, I called this person "my sun." That's why on that piece of paper I drew a big picture of the sun and next to it I wrote:

I'd like to meet someone very special to share my travels with.

Little did I know that later the same day a blonde Englishman would write a very similar message in silver ink on a purple butterfly.

As the event unfolded, I settled into the extraordinary rhythm of artistic over-stimulation as every day seemed to improve upon the last. Finally, a few minutes before midnight on New Year's Eve, hundreds of people gathered around the little lake that acts as one of the focal points of what, by now, we were all calling "Woodfordia." Each person received a candle, and at midnight a strange, eerie calm descended over the entire camp as all the music stages fell silent. One hundred thousand people in total silence creates a very special atmosphere and standing motionless amongst them, I remember thinking:

My sun must be here.

The next morning, having finished serving coffee to all the performers, I was strolling toward a singing workshop that was being run by the Chilean performer Nano Stern. Passing the main office tent, I glanced at the notice board hoping to find a lift to Sydney, where I was planning to find a job. An unusual little flyer grabbed my attention:

Free sailing for happy people: looking for crew for a sailing trip to Sydney. No experience required, but a positive disposition essential.

I quickly scribbled the number down on a serviette and carried on with my day. Little did I know that this number would change my life.

A few days later, the skipper invited all the potential crew members to a meeting. He seemed like a nice enough guy and I signed on as crew. I was so happy (and admittedly, slightly overwhelmed) by the thought of ocean sailing that I completely failed to notice that the skipper was wearing a bright yellow t-shirt with a smiling sun emblazoned on it.

I arrived in Bundaberg with my little backpack in the early
days of 2010 and moved aboard *Marutji*, a 34-ft steel sloop
designed by the legendary EG Van de Stadt and built in
Australia out of steel. We set off in perfect conditions down
the Burnett River and out to sea. Unfortunately, these
perfect conditions did not persist, and by the end of the day,
I was quite shell-shocked. Having only sailed in the
relatively flat seas of the Adriatic, I was not prepared for
the rolling swell of the Pacific Ocean. When we finally
dropped anchor at the entrance to Hervey Bay, I was
practically packing my bag to leave. However, Rick (the
skipper) explained that the week ahead would be spent in
the still waters of the Great Sandy Strait which is protected
from the swell by a chain of islands and is more like an
inland delta. So I decided to stay. And stay I did. Very soon

I would fall in love with Rick and *Marutji*, and the three of us would cover many thousands of miles together.

Somewhere along this journey of sail and romance, we realized that this lifestyle rather suited us. *Marutji*, on the other hand, was less well suited to extended cruising so we decided to take advantage of the ridiculously strong Australian dollar to sell her and go shopping for our new floating home overseas.

After an unsuccessful (yet enjoyable) search through Indonesia, Thailand, and Malaysia, we found our new home in Mexico. In July 2011, we moved aboard *Calypso*, and for the next three years we sailed the west coast of

Mexico and her islands while we prepared her for ocean crossing.

In those years, we actually worked more than we sailed, and the relentless nature of the preparations began to take a toll upon us. Whenever we thought the work was almost over, something else would pop up that needed addressing. At one point we even started to wonder if we had bought the wrong boat. After a particular run of disappointing discoveries, Rick eventually lost confidence in *Calypso* and, in a pique of ire, decided to sell her.

We found a buyer very quickly. A survey and test sail were completed with flying colors and a $10,000 deposit handed over with the balance due in four weeks. In the meantime, we agreed to haul her out of the water and make certain changes to her, as well as move all our stuff off her. As we had no other place to live, we had to hire a little storage unit for all our luggage. Our good friends, Tim and Meredith, allowed us to live aboard their boat *Lucy* while they were back in the States. As we were hauling *Calypso* out of the water, we realized how dumb we had been to sell her after completing nearly all the projects and how close she really was to being ready. We now saw our decision to sell as a mistake - a petulant reaction caused by temporary frustration and all out of proportion to the situation.

I immediately burst into tears. That was the end of all our plans and dreams. Rick was sad too, but it was too late to change our minds. The deal had already been done, and both Rick and I are too old-fashioned to go back on even a handshake, let alone a signed contract.

Well, several payment deadlines came and went, and we were beginning to dare to hope that the buyer had changed his mind. It was a very distant hope so, in the meantime, we carried on working in dry dock to complete the rest of the little improvements that were part of the contract's conditions of sale.

Amongst other things, the buyer had asked us to apply new antifouling to the hull (this is the special paint one applies to the underside of the boat to prevent marine growth). So, there I was on New Year's Eve applying the stinky, toxic black goop and I have to tell you, I felt pretty sorry for myself.

I certainly wasn't working to our usual standard. The boat was no longer mine, plus the buyer was messing us around with the final payment, so my motivation was more or less zero as I moped about slapping paint around like a drunk post-impressionist. I was just mixing up some more paint when I heard the phone ring and saw Rick disappear into the bowels of the boat to find the wretched thing and answer it. Ten minutes later, he appeared before me with two glasses of twelve-year-old single malt Scottish whiskey in his hands and a stupid grin on his face.

"At 9 a.m.?" I asked slightly confused.

"We have to toast our new boat!"

"What?! Which one?" I asked, glancing around the half-empty yard.

"This one," said Rick, knocking a whiskey glass against my freshly painted hull. "The buyer has changed his mind; *Calypso* is ours again!"

Oh, how happy were we! We got to keep the boat and with the money from the deposit were able to finish the jobs that had previously motivated us to sell her. I was intensely relieved. I got straight back to painting but this time with an entirely different attitude. Rather than slapping on the goop like a disillusioned house painter, I was now the Michelangelo of antifouling.

The next day we celebrated the start of the New Year with a nice Mexican dinner. Rick raised a Corona and toasted:

"To *Calypso* and all who sail in her!"

"Where are we going?" I asked.

He thought about it for a moment and said:

"The boat is ready and so are we. Let's sail to the South Pacific!"

The die was cast.

The journey

If you look at the globe between America and Australia, you see only blue. One has to pick up a more detailed map to notice the thousands of little dots of land scattered across the oversized blue canvas of the world's largest and emptiest ocean. One of these little dots is Hiva Oa in the Marquesas Islands, which we picked as our first landfall in French Polynesia. But there were still 3,000 nautical miles and a month of sailing between us and this idyllic safe harbor. Thirty long days without land, thirty days floating on that sometimes flat, sometimes very wavy line which separates the sky from the sea.

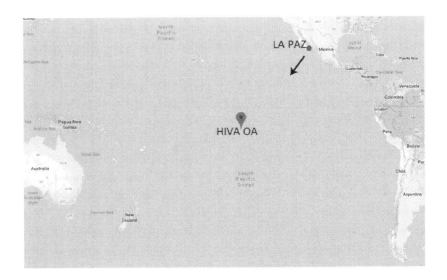

A mixture of excitement and fear woke us up very early. When I opened my eyes, Rick was already looking at me.

"Are you ready for the Pacific Ocean?" he asked me quietly.

I smiled and whispered, "I am!"

So, with butterflies in our stomachs, we raised the anchor and sailed toward the rest of the world.

April 2, 2014: Farewell

Our first day of sailing is slowly coming to an end as we travel toward the tip of the Baja peninsula where we will join the open ocean. I am sitting in the cockpit and wondering how these sails can move us with such a light breath - I really cannot call it wind. The sun is setting, and *Calypso* is moving at about two knots on a glassy sea. I look at the beaches, the peaks, and the islands around me and I quietly say my farewells.

The silence is profound. I can hear the splashes of stingrays jumping, but they are too far away for me to see them. Their acrobatic jumps with double spins kept us amused many a hot night in Mexico. I will miss them. I like to think they came to say goodbye.

Earlier, when we were raising the spinnaker, I also saw a familiar hairy nose swimming alongside. I used to confuse sea lions with dolphins but have since learned to recognize their specific movements and behaviors. I find them most amusing when they sunbathe. They spread their flippers, lie on their backs, and show their tummy to the sun. They are so chilled; they only lack dark sunglasses and a cocktail with an umbrella.

I am slightly envious that Rick saw whales during his watch. The Sea of Cortez may be lacking vegetation on land, but the abundance of marine life certainly makes up for it.

The small fishing villages of Baja California are slipping past our starboard side. In our wake is the fishing village of San Evaristo where we have spent many wonderful moments amongst the hardworking people who live there, including the now legendary (on *Calypso* at least) New Year's Eve party of 2012. We had arrived in San Evaristo Bay on December 31st and had hardly got the anchor down before somebody rowed out to invite us to the revelries.

The food was typically Mexican, with grilled chicken, beans, and the mandatory mountain of tortillas. We sat under the palm tree roof and huddled around the grill to warm up. After emptying our plates for the third time, we jumped on the back of a pickup and drove for some time along a bumpy road with the wind in our hair and the sand in our eyes, finally stopping in front of a big house full of people and lively music. At the door the owner welcomed us with typical Mexican hospitality.

"Mi casa es su casa." (My home is your home.)

And what a party we found inside! The whole village was gathered in one enormous room. One corner was occupied by the older women, the opposite with men sporting sombreros. The younger villagers were dancing, and the children ran around making mischief.

It was a very cold night, so we joined the dancers to warm up. After a while we sat down, but the village women were not going to let us off so lightly and gestured that we should get back up and continue dancing. As soon as we complied, they cheered loudly and seemed satisfied. Their wonderful, toothless smiles more than compensated for our aching limbs.

At midnight, it was time for hugging. The hugs we received that night were so sincere and hearty that we still feel a certain warmth whenever we remember them.

The party finally came to an end and we hopped onto the pickup truck for the drive back to the beach in the pitch dark, swerving violently to avoid cactuses and potholes. Our fellow passengers, the now slightly drunk villagers, dragged out some colorful wigs which provoked general giggling, especially amongst the children. We were laughing and dancing and just simply enjoying being so happy goofing around with these simple props.

Deposited on the beach, we waved our final farewells and launched our trusty kayak into the gentle waters of the bay to paddle the short distance back to *Calypso*, which was not hard to spot, being the only boat in the cove. Halfway between the beach and the boat, we stopped paddling, but our kayak kept gently sliding through the bioluminescent water. The sea around us was completely still, thousands of stars gleamed in the sky, and in the distance we could still hear Mexican melodies. It was an unforgettable moment of peace. It was the most beautiful New Year's Eve.

In the following years, we returned to San Evaristo a number of times and made many good friends there. One time we arrived to bring a mountain of academic supplies for their elementary school that had been donated by my fellow Slovenian countrymen. Another time to seek protection from very strong northerly winds. Other times just to visit and drink beer. Every time we raised the sails to leave, someone in the village would ring a bell, blow a horn, or call us on the VHF radio:

"Adios, *Calypso*, buena suerte!" (Goodbye, *Calypso*, good luck!)

Mexico touched us deeply. Its people are warm, hearty, and happy. Every occasion is an excuse for celebration. Lively music is omnipresent, and people greet you with a sincere smile and a firm handshake. Although they do not have much, they are generous. Although they are not particularly academic, they are very curious, and they know a lot. I had some high-level debates with a taxi driver who I later learned to be illiterate. I know I will miss these wonderful people.

We have spent almost three years in the company of Mexican fishermen, stingrays, and sea lions, and today we are finally saying goodbye. I am not without regret, but it is time for a new page in our ship's log. The wind seems to agree and finally picks up. The sails are filling and *Calypso* glides onwards toward new horizons.

April 3, 2014: Courage

It is 2 a.m., time for my first night watch. A full moon lights the night sky and a tired shearwater (mutton bird) is stealing a ride on the rail. I tried to photograph his dark outline with the moon in the background, but the waves are shaking the camera way too much to get anything useful out of it. Sometimes I find myself wondering if some scenes deliberately resist being caught by camera in order to preserve their uniqueness. Perhaps we look at them with different eyes if we know that we have only a few seconds to ingest all their beauty. I cannot remember how many times I have tried to photograph bioluminescence (the plankton that glows in the dark) only to get a result that looks like somebody sneezed on a blackboard. Only once I realized the impossibility of the task was I free to simply enjoy this unique show.

It isn't easy to describe the phenomenon of sailing in dense bioluminescence. Perhaps best described as sailing in a starry sky, the scene becomes even more unreal when dolphins whoosh past the boat like glittering torpedoes. But even at anchor, the water can be full of light. It is fun to stir the water by hand and make it shine. Sometimes I grab a handful of water and pour it from one hand to the other to admire the diamond dust. I also like to submerge a line in the sea, because it will glow with fairy dust for quite some time after I pull it back on deck.

I love night watches, especially the ones like tonight, when the sea is calm and there is no traffic at all. The Sea of

Cortez is known for being empty at night; only small fishing boats gather near the coast.

That's why I am particularly surprised to see a single, strong white light off our starboard bow at around four in the morning. My heart starts pounding, and I immediately turn on the radar to check the distance between us. And what do I see? Nothing! The light is so bright; it must be fairly close, and yet there are no ships on the radar. I scurry back on deck - the light is still there, and I am sailing straight toward it! It is horrible not knowing how far away it is. The light is about one inch above the horizon, which means that the boat is close, too close!

I have to do something and do it right now. I decide to turn toward land, fifty degrees to starboard, so I will definitely avoid her if she keeps her course. I am too nervous to go down below so I stay in the cockpit and keep a wary eye on the mysterious light in the middle of the sea. The moment I am sure we are safe, I'll turn us back on course, but right now I am heading straight toward land. I stare into the light and get lost in my own thoughts. Just as I am drifting into the arena of over-introspection, a large, high cloud covers the sky and the bright light disappears. I am quite embarrassed when I realize that for the last two hours I have been trying to outrun a star. Rick is going to have a good laugh.

At dawn I make myself a cup of green tea and go to the cockpit to admire the birth of a new day. I take the first sip, look toward land, and I am instantly shocked. There is an entire army of motorboats coming straight for us at full speed! After the initial shock, I deduce that they are sport fishing boats coming from the touristy village of Cabo San Lucas (the huge fishing rods and over-powered outboard motors gave them away). I count more than fifty boats! Thankfully it is daylight - I may have had a heart attack if I had seen this many blips on the radar screen.

I remember now seeing a drone picture of this bay with its myriad of milling boats and wondering what kind of event had got so many vessels so excited. But obviously this scene happens nearly every day as part of the sport fishing tourist industry. What I still don't understand is why the hell do they need to run right at us? It is a big ocean! Probably they are just curious about this totally becalmed floaty thing with floppy red sails.

The scene is actually quite comical. I am not entirely sure what to expect. They get closer and closer, and I keep staring at them. Surprisingly, they do not stop to say hi, nor do they slow down. Instead, they fly past us at full speed. One barely misses the stern; others almost run into the bowsprit, each of them leaving a large wake behind and rolling *Calypso* one way and then the next. If they had taken the time to glance in our direction, they would have seen a sleepy gargoyle in her pajamas waving at them. Maybe they would have thought I was greeting them, but I was actually swearing because they made me spill my tea.

Cabo San Lucas is the most southerly point of the Baja California peninsula and the gateway to the Pacific. Here we will decide whether we are really going to cross the Pacific Ocean or turn south toward Costa Rica. We know very well that the journey will be long and demanding.

Often scary. I already know that seasickness, as always, will make me wonder why I am doing this to myself.

We do not feel the need to prove anything to anyone, so we will ultimately do whatever pleases us. On the other hand, we have been preparing *Calypso* for ocean sailing for almost three years, and if we were to give up now, all our efforts would feel somewhat pointless.

After a long debate, Rick asks the crucial question.

"What will we do if we don't go?"

The question floats in the air for a while and remains unanswered.

So, we are going.

We have invested a lot of time, effort, and money in this dream. It would be stupid to give it up based on a little fear and trepidation.

The boat is well prepared and so is the crew. Some fear remains, of course, because there will always be factors over which we have no control. A happy conclusion to an ocean crossing requires good preparation and planning, but a bit of luck should never be turned down. I have a small booklet in my locker onboard *Calypso*, a gift from Milanka Lange Lipovec who was the first Slovenian woman to sail around the world. On the inside cover, her personal dedication says:

Luck is on the side of the brave.

I know it is not always true, but I do hope that somewhere in the bilge, amongst all our other supplies, we have remembered to pack a good supply of courage.

April 4, 2014: Disappointment

When I was trying to envision this voyage, I imagined glittering seas, tropical temperatures, and naked sunbathing. The real picture, however, is fundamentally different. For the last two days, we have had grey and cold conditions more typical of the North Sea than the Pacific. The temperature is more polar than tropical. Despite cowering behind the sprayhood, I still need to wrap myself in wooly socks, hat, and full foul weather gear in order not to freeze to death. Strangely, the more we sail south, the colder it gets. This is an upside-down world! We have already crossed the 23rd parallel and therefore officially entered the tropics, supposedly the world of eternal summer. If the temperature continues to drop at this rate, we shall be on iceberg watch within the week.

At least we finally have some northerlies, which has slightly improved the atmosphere on board, but the wind also brings steep waves that collide with the southerly swell. *Calypso* is creaking from pitching and rolling violently in the confused seas. Slowly it is getting to me, so I take a Sturgeron, my beloved seasickness pill. I know myself well enough to know when I need it.

I really do not fancy cooking. Today I ate one pear, five crackers, one carrot and a little bowl of rice. The fridge is full of fresh vegetables which will probably rot where they lie if the sea continues to be so relentless.

Most of my friends wished me good luck before leaving with the word: "Enjoy!"

So far, there is little sign of enjoyment, but in all honesty, I did not expect anything different. I had read enough sailors' accounts of this voyage to spare me the comfort of such naivety. I have yet to read one that is free of examples of exhaustion and lack of sleep, so I tried to prepare myself psychologically for both.

My fear of tiredness is actually greater than my fear of storms. I am a person who needs at least eight hours of sleep for normal operation. Unlike Rick, who seems to be able to function on nothing at all, I get serious headaches and dizziness if I do not get a reasonable facsimile of my full quota.

I know the sea well enough to know what to expect, but I am beginning to have doubts about myself. I know that at some point, like it or not, I will have to get up in the middle of the night and fight with bad weather. Will I make it? After four years of sailing together, I know that we can solve even the most seemingly hopeless of problems at sea. But I do wonder whether we can be so invincible at the jagged end of exhaustion.

While the boat is at sea, someone must be constantly on watch. For boats with a number of crew, this is no big deal, but it can be a bit more demanding for couples. The majority of couples have a system that requires a change of watch every three hours or so. Such a short watch time is good for the watchkeeper because the time passes relatively quickly, but for us this is not an option. If somebody wakes me up after three hours, they had better be ready for trouble. After such little sleep I become an angry lioness with very little sense of humor. I cry, scream, scratch, and bite.

Rick tried it only once, after which he wisely decided to find a better solution. So we now split the night in half. Eight o'clock is my natural time to sleep on both land and sea. Such an early night often attracts scorn amongst my more party-orientated friends on land, but at sea, it makes me very popular indeed. Rick wakes me up at 2 a.m. and sleeps until eight in the morning. This allows both of us to get a good six hours of deep sleep that allows the body to get a proper re-boot. We usually have breakfast together, then it is my time to rest until lunch. If I cannot sleep, I watch a movie or read a book. In the afternoon, I take care of the boat and Rick rests. So far, this system works perfectly and there are no signs of exhaustion.

It is almost three o'clock. Time for my afternoon watch. I get out of bed, grab my headphones, and head to the cockpit. I look around and, for the first time, there is no land in sight. Just blue everywhere.

I am not sure exactly why (maybe it's the music in my ears or because we have finally sailed out into the open ocean), but an immense sense of happiness overtakes me. I feel that I am exactly where I want to be. Exactly where I belong. I have a good look at all this water around me and then close my eyes. I take a long breath and fill my lungs with ocean air to a depth that can only be truly achieved at sea.

The sun finally breaks through the clouds, the wind begins to die down, and I begin to thaw. As soon as it gets a little warmer, I'll grab a bucket of ocean water and wash my hair.

I am beginning to hope that my friends are right - this journey may well be enjoyable.

April 5, 2014: Discomfort

I woke up to a gray and sad morning. The wind has picked up again in the night and with it, of course, the waves. The average swell is now about ten feet (3m) high and occasionally a series of giants arrive from nowhere. Just looking at them makes me shiver. The radio informs us that they are the result of a big storm raging off Alaska. Although I am glad that the bad weather is far away, it does not really help much. The big swell can travel very far and make life pretty difficult for us. *Calypso* is fighting hard, but every big wave is like running into a wall. The wall of water stops the boat dead, and we fly forward, up, right, or left. Everything needs to be done with one hand, the other hand being occupied with gripping and generally preventing myself flying through the boat with the speed of Superman (but with much less likelihood of achieving anything for the betterment of humanity). But life goes on even though I would like to stop it, at least for a minute or two.

It would be nice to disconnect, disappear, go far, far away from this discomfort. I wish I could magically appear in my family home in Sistiana. I would lie amongst flowers, walk on the freshly mowed grass, look at the crisp, spring sky, and climb my favorite tree. But I cannot. Like it or not, I am on a boat that bounces like a frenzied horse, and there is literally nothing I can do about it. So I resign myself to try to live more or less normally. The upshot of this is that I decide to cut my toenails.

Seriously? What is wrong with me? Do I really have nothing better to do?

It took me more than half an hour to do such a simple task. Had I known how much effort it would take, I would probably have done something less stupid. The fact that I still have the standard quota of toes is a remarkable achievement indeed.

Yesterday I wrote a short message via ham radio to my sister Tanja, trying to describe life aboard. Like many non-sailors, Tanja's image of the sailing life is quite idyllic. Over the years I have tried to dissuade her of that image, but I realized the extent of my failure to do so when her reply came back suggesting that I might try to shift my bad mood by 'going for a little swim' - an act which would have resulted in near certain death in these conditions.

Imagine having to do all your daily jobs while riding a horse. Can you see yourself brushing your teeth on a trotting horse? Or changing your underwear, making a coffee, or writing some emails?

I know that many people find it difficult to imagine that simply lying in bed can be a challenging task. But if I wish to have any chance of sleeping well, I have to squeeze into a corner, wedge my head between two pillows, and wear some earplugs to mute the relentless noise of the waves and tortured creaking of the boat as she attempts to rise and fall in these ugly crossed seas.

I never imagined that I would someday need to develop a new technique even for drinking water from a glass. This is how it goes: I get the glass close to my mouth, I wait for the wave to come and go and then quickly sip before the next one arrives. Even so I sometimes pour more water on my shirt than in my mouth.

But wait! Cooking is even more fun! The cooker is gimbaled (free to swing) so that the burners are always level to the earth's surface. This makes it the only safe place to put a bowl, a plate, or a carton of eggs. If I put them anywhere else, they will soon become airborne, destination unknown. The swinging stove is certainly a fantastic addition to a blue water boat, but cooking on it also requires a new set of skills. For example, if I want to mix the boiling pasta, I must first carefully approach the violently swinging pot and then use judicious timing with the wooden spoon to stir whilst holding on to something solid, lest I be dumped on top of the whole thing, bruised, scalded, and, most likely, on fire.

Since I knew that this would be the case, I prepared a lot of food in advance. As Rick is totally immune to sea sickness, I am now forced to watch him happily chomp his way through it like a self-satisfied little pig whilst I nibble on a dry cracker.

Do not even get me started on the subject of toilets. It takes me at least ten minutes to gather the energy and motivation to go, as being downstairs (or 'below' as we sailors say) only increases my nausea. Subsequently, I always try to put it off as long as I can. The head (bathroom) is so small that I can steady myself by pressing both feet into the opposite wall and holding onto the bowl. This helps a lot, but when *Calypso* falls down a particularly big wave, I still get thrown into the air. So I prefer to pee overboard, which on our boat is quite easy thanks to the boomkin. This is a little platform that extends aft from the stern of classic boats like *Calypso*. You rarely see them on modern yachts, but they are a godsend in a seaway when you need a pee.

Changing clothes is another drama. If a big wave hits at the right moment, I inevitably find myself on the ground with my feet in the air. These are the moments when I cannot help but think of all those lovely people who keep saying how much they envy me and my idyllic life afloat.

Of course they envy me. They think my life is one continuous sunbathing session on the foredeck (occasionally interrupted when Rick brings me a coconut), swimming in dream anchorages, watching the sunset with a cocktail in my hand, and romantically strolling on white beaches.

To be fair, this is largely my fault. When I show my photos of sandy islands and endless sunshine, I create a fairytale that is a long way from reality. When everything goes wrong, or I feel sick or on edge of tears, I tend not to reach for the camera. Instead I simply hope that the awful moment will pass as quickly as possible, which explains why there is a fairly large piece missing from my photographic record. If ever found, it would be a gallery of bad weather, torn sails, seasickness, cockroaches, rats, dusty boatyards, and so on. Such moments always remain in the shade. Perhaps they should.

Despite having confessed partial culpability, I still get slightly miffed when somebody says, "I envy you so much!"

I bet that, in this moment, none of those who envy me so much would like to switch their comfortable life for mine. I have most certainly had enough! I'm glad that it is Rick's watch and I can now strap myself into my berth, put my ear plugs in, and shut out this gray, cold, and frightening reality for a while.

....

Okay, forget all that. I have just awakened and it is as if we have sailed into another world. The weather is glorious. The sun is shining; the wind has abated. The sky is clear to all points of the horizon, and a fair wind is nudging us in the right direction. There is still some residual swell from the storm which will take a while to die down, but *Calypso* has stopped moaning and groaning and no longer feels as if she is about to break up. Rick is looking very smug in the cockpit and I love sailing again.

After a few days, life on board becomes blissfully repetitive: six hours of sleep down below, six hours on watch on deck, six hours of sleep, six hours of watch. The only thing that interrupts the routine of daily life is the evening SSB radio net. At 7 p.m. all the sailboats crossing the Pacific meet at an agreed channel on the single sideband radio to report our positions and have a chat. In addition to the exact coordinates and navigation data, we also report the weather and anything special that happened. This section is mainly about gear failures and fishing. When we hear a familiar voice, I always invite that crew to stay on the frequency after the net to have a chat. Only those who have experienced loneliness in the middle of the ocean can understand how important it is to hear a friendly voice, even though it may be coming from thousands of miles away.

Tonight I was hoping to be able to contact Eric and Charlotte Kaufman from *Rebel Heart*. They left two weeks before us and the last we heard, they were experiencing some bad weather. We have been friends with Charlotte and Eric for some time. We first met them in La Cruz in Mexico when we paddled over to say hi because they have exactly the same boat as ours. I mean exactly the same, down to the color, which is quite a coincidence because these boats are quite rare. I have been thinking about Charlotte quite often these days. The bad weather we just came through was difficult enough, but Charlotte also has two kids to care for. The eldest is three years old and can pretty much take care of herself, but she also has a one-year-old who often needs to be in Charlotte's arms.

Tonight, the voices on the evening net sound particularly nervous. Everyone is reporting huge waves, a boat that has torn her sails and another that has been dismasted. One crew decided to turn back, another not to leave Mexico at all. In the end someone also mentions *Rebel Heart*. Relieved to be finally getting some news of our friends, I crank up the volume and lean into the radio. But the relief does not last long. The net controller reports that the youngest daughter had health problems and the parents decided to send out an emergency call. Apparently, a US Coast Guard helicopter responded and lowered a doctor onto the boat. We'll find out more tomorrow. I hope they are all right.

In the meantime, the sun has set, and it is time for me to go off watch. I hesitate to admit how much I enjoy squeezing into my bunk every evening and escaping into the world of dreams for several hours. The real world, which roars and shouts, is way too scary. The angry sea becomes even scarier in the dark. When images disappear, only sounds remain; creaking, beating, blowing, and roaring compete to see which will scare me the most. I cannot see the waves anymore; I just hear them strafing the boat. They hit hard and angry like a strong slap. I shiver each time. I am scared. I lay in my bunk listening to them and quietly hope to survive the next one.

April 6, 2014: Strength

I cannot recall such a dark night for a long time. The wind and waves have picked up. It is too scary outside, so I stay at the navigation table where I can check on the instruments to see if we are sailing in the right direction. I only pop my head out every fifteen minutes or so to scan the horizon for shipping. Although I took a pill against seasickness, I feel decidedly iffy. Writing and reading are out of the question, so I put on the headphones and listen to music. This really helps. Although I am still wedged in the corner staring into space, the music helps the time pass more quickly. Happy melodies manage to slightly smother the frightening sounds of the angry ocean.

After the first hour of my watch, when I was already feeling pleased that there were only five left, something unexpected happened. Even though the swell has been on the beam (the side) all day long, at three o'clock in the morning, it decides to surprise us. A huge steep wave suddenly comes from behind. It hits our stern with an immense force, completely floods the cockpit and flies straight through the cabin, landing with extreme prejudice on the bunk where Rick is resting. The poor guy had just finally managed to fall asleep before this column of cold water jetted onto him. The amount of water was huge and, in an instant, he is as completely soaked as if he had fallen into the sea. The whole thing is so sudden and unexpected; he jumped up with big eyes, completely drenched and confused. Despite the initial scare, the scene is quite comical really, but Rick is still in the shock of it and sees the whole thing differently.

"I hate this boat, I hate the sea, and I hate this trip!" he shouts while drying his hair with a towel.

I quickly prepare a dry bunk on the other side of the saloon and bring him dry clothes. When he lies down again, I stroke him for some time and manage to calm him down.

"I know you hate this trip. I am not loving it either. If you want, we can turn around. It is not too late. But we'll decide tomorrow. Now close your eyes and sleep, my sweetheart."

I am unusually calm and confident, completely without fear. Somewhere deep inside, I know that we cannot both give up at the same time. In these last few days, I was very weak and unmotivated. Rick saw how difficult it was for me and tried to relieve me as much as he could by having longer watches and constantly reassuring me. But when he needed respite from the scary ocean, it pulled from me a strength I did not even know I had. Much later, a journalist writing about us said that our strength was not that we never quit, but we never quit at the same time. I did not realize it then, but when I saw it written, it had the unmistakable ring of truth about it.

At 7 a.m., a shy ray of sunshine finally pierces the dark clouds. There is still a very large swell from the north, but the wind has calmed down. I hope for some more sunshine today, so I can dry out the pillows, towels, clothes, and captain which are still soaked from last night's exciting events.

The big wave that showered Rick in the middle of the night also dealt a fatal blow to our electric autopilot. The first victim of this trip is therefore known. To be fair, this failure is not totally surprising. We expected this to happen sooner or later as electronics and salt water simply do not mix. That's precisely why a year ago we installed a mechanical, wind-powered, self-steering system. It is a remarkable device that is simple, repairable, and consumes no energy. We named it Homer.

But this morning, Homer is being difficult too. I know that it is not a big deal - probably just a line that got tangled up in the steering compartment, but I don't want to wake Rick up just yet. I take the helm and let him sleep; it is not difficult to hand steer *Calypso* for a while.

Rick wakes up at eight, has a cup of tea and then appears in the cockpit. I can tell he is not in the best mood but is trying to shrug it off. We try to engage the self-steering, but it is still being difficult. Everything seems fine to look at it, so the problem must be in the steering compartment. Bummer. That means emptying the cockpit locker. Rick begins pulling lines, fenders, buckets, and anchors into the cockpit while I continue hand steering.

It always surprises me when I hear of sailors who go to sea with only an electric autopilot. I really wouldn't dare. When it breaks down (and sooner or later it will), it is too complicated to be fixed en route, so each of us would have to steer for twelve hours per day, regardless of wind, rain, or waves. No thanks.

On such a long passage, there is quite enough work to do without adding steering to the list. If, after trimming and shortening sails, doing navigation, cooking, checking the horizon and the radar, filling the logbook, listening to weather forecasts, eating, taking pictures, fishing, sleeping, and occasionally vomiting, there is still some spare time left, I really don't want to spend it steering. I would rather have an extra nap.

Rick is head-first in the cockpit locker in a position more typically found in a yoga manual than on a boat. Drills, hammers, and various tools all disappear into the bowels of the boat, but eventually he wins! The wind vane takes over the steering again and I can finally let go of the wheel. I knew he would fix it. He always manages to fix everything. He has that mix of skill and stubbornness that is very useful on a boat.

The clock says it is already noon, which means that this repair has eaten into my watch and I have now been on duty for ten long hours. Rick kindly offers to extend his watch so I can sleep for at least four hours. But before I go to bed, we still have to solve a minor problem with the genoa furling system. One of us must go onto the bowsprit. This is the stick that extends forward of the bow and is the most exposed part of the boat, where the bouncing is at its wildest, and you know in advance that sooner or later a big wave will drench you from head to toe. Historically, many sailors have been washed overboard whilst working on the bowsprit, and it is easy to see how it earned its nickname, 'the widow maker.'

Usually I avoid the bowsprit like bubonic plague, but today I surprise myself by announcing that I will do whatever needs to be done. I think I know why I have so uncharacteristically volunteered for this onerous task. Firstly, my morale is high because the weather has improved, the waves have begun to lie down, and Rick has fixed the wind vane self-steering. Secondly, I get the impression from Rick's outburst last night that he is feeling the pressure a bit more than I imagined, and I feel the need to help him by taking on as much as I can.

I had not really appreciated how much easier it is to be the crew than the captain. Rick has a great sense of this responsibility, which must add to his stress. He often mentions that he was never afraid when he was sailing single-handed. Now he feels the responsibility of bringing me back to shore alive and in one piece. He says that the most frightening thought is that one day he'd have to face my mum and tell her that I am gone. I totally understand his fear, but there is little I can do to alleviate it other than try and take care of myself and take on as many of the tasks and responsibilities I am capable of removing from his shoulders.

So I gather my courage and crawl to the bowsprit.

Before I begin this task, I attach myself with a double safety harness so I will have free hands and not worry about falling into the ocean. I sit down on the bowsprit as if I were sitting on a horse, my legs dangling in the air and occasionally dipping into the sea. I am absolutely, utterly not thinking about getting sick. I try not to think of the bow plunging into the ocean and taking me for a little submarine ride. My eyes and my thoughts are focused solely on the work I have to accomplish. I slowly unfasten the knot, unwind the line, furl the sail by hand, and make sure it does not run out. I have to stop once and crawl back to the cockpit on my knees to collect some pliers, but I eventually solve the problem. Overall, I spent more than half an hour on the bouncy bowsprit, and only after the work was done did I realize that I was not seasick in the slightest. I feel great, even without medicines. It is day five and I finally have my sea legs.

The afternoon is much more peaceful, no surprises, although the weather is still very unsettled.

In the evening the net controller reports that the boat *Rebel Heart* is all right. They are handling the problems with the rudder, the daughter is out of danger, and apparently they are sailing back to Mexico. This decision definitely surprises us. Sailing back means 900 miles of beating into the wind against the swell and the current. Although the journey to Polynesia is twice as long, it is also twice as easy. I wonder whether Eric stayed alone on the boat or if they are still all together. I would like to hear from them and ask if we can help in any way. Maybe they can wait for us to sail together if we're not too far.

"Tomorrow I will try to find out their position," I say to myself before I fall asleep.

April 7, 2014: Sadness

In Mexico we would usually start the day by tuning into the Amigo Net on the SSB radio. Until today I didn't even think of checking if we can still hear it, but I do and we can. Great! I will tune in while Rick is on watch in the cockpit enjoying a windy but sunny morning. This net is very valuable because a weather forecasting expert gives advice to boats all over the Pacific Coast. We are quite far from the coast already, but close to the Socorro Islands, so I try my luck anyway. To my great surprise, he tells me that today he prepared a special forecast for this area, at the request of the sailing boat *Isleña*. That's our friends, Sam and David! How nice to hear that they are here! The radio controller connects us so we can have a chat after the net.

"Can I do anything else for you, Jasna? Would you like to contact somebody?"

I jump to the opportunity and ask:

"Do you have the last known position of the sailing vessel *Rebel Heart* and maybe some news about their situation?"

He tells me what I already know: that a helicopter arrived with medical help, that the child was stable, but nevertheless evacuated. We all wonder if they only evacuated the one-year-old but I am pretty sure Charlotte would go with her. But what about her sister? Did she stay with Eric on the boat or did she leave with her mum? So, is Eric now alone? I am very worried, and I would like to help him if only I knew exactly where he was.

A strong signal cuts in from the background noise with new information.

"The Navy evacuated the whole family. I repeat, the whole family is now on the ship of the US Navy. Everyone is alive and well."

The news is comforting, but at the same time I feel a sense of disquiet as I think I know what is coming next. The voice continues the report:

"Unfortunately, they had to scuttle the boat. I repeat, the family is saved; the boat has been sunk."

I am speechless. I need a second to calm down before telling Rick the sad news. We are both shocked.

Last year we were preparing our boat for sailing across the Pacific Ocean with many of our friends doing the same passage. In the end, a serious engine problem forced us to remain in Mexico and delay our departure until the following year. It was hard to wave goodbye to all our friends, but that is part of the sailing life. Nevertheless, we followed their progress on the radio and read their blogs regularly, so sometimes it felt like we were with them.

This year is different. Amongst almost a hundred yachts crossing the Pacific, the only other boat we knew well was *Rebel Heart*. I cannot get my head around the fact that I will not see them in Tahiti and that I will never again see *Rebel Heart* because she rests on the bottom of the Pacific Ocean.

I realize that *Rebel Heart* is not the first boat to ever sink and she most certainly won't be the last. Nevertheless, I am deeply saddened by the scuttling of such a sea-worthy boat because I know very well how much effort, work, and money Eric and Charlotte have put into her.

When one buys a boat, it is not advisable to simply slip the mooring lines and head out into the ocean any more than it makes sense to head for the church the moment one meets someone they fancy. Although some do it, it still does not mean that it is wise. I know some people who have sailed the ocean with a recently bought boat. Some were lucky and are now writing books about how sailing around the world is a piece of cake. Others were less lucky. They cannot write books because they are gone. Some trust their lucky star, but I prefer not to ask too much from the celestial bodies. I do not want to test the limits of their patience. *Rebel Heart* was as well prepared as any boat that ever put to sea. It is almost unthinkable (not to mention grossly unfair) that she now resides in Davy Jones' locker whilst many crews on far less seaworthy boats are drinking rum on a tropical island, claiming that ocean passages are easy and wondering what all the fuss is about.

When I read books about ocean sailing, I repeatedly encounter the claim that no one should cross an ocean without first living aboard for at least two years and sailing short and long distances. I fully agree with this. Only after two years of intense sailing and trying to break things can I say that I finally trust *Calypso*.

During this time, we got to know all of her systems in detail and sailed her in a wide variety of situations. From the day we bought her, we have done so much work on her that we know each and every hidden corner of her, her weaknesses, and her strengths.

We seldom hire a professional to do any work for us, unless the job needs equipment we do not have or could not reasonably be expected to acquire and stow on the boat. There are several reasons for this.

The first is, of course, the financial implications. Every penny we save by doing the work ourselves we can put to use somewhere else on the boat. More important than the financial saving is the reassurance of the quality of the work. Nobody has more of a vested interest in the quality of a repair than the person whose life depends upon its integrity. Last but not least, if we do the work ourselves, we learn new skills which will surely come in handy on a tiny island in the middle of nowhere where there are few people of any description, let alone marine professionals.

It was often back-breaking work, but it didn't matter because we never lost sight of the ultimate goal. My goal had the shape of a sandy beach with a hammock swinging between palm trees and an icy cocktail with a decorative umbrella. I do not know what form Eric and Charlotte's dream took, but it almost certainly sank with the boat.

I am very sad for them, but their story also makes me think. I know lots of sailing families. I know mothers who gave birth on a boat and children who have never lived in a house. I have no doubts that raising kids aboard is possible (and an excellent choice if you ask me), but taking toddlers on ocean passages does seem too much like hard work for a lazy sailor like me. Looking after the boat, myself, and my doofus boyfriend is quite enough work, thank you very much.

After breakfast, I lie down but I cannot sleep. I cannot erase the image of Eric watching his boat sink. I wonder if he had to sink her himself or if he left that particularly unpleasant task to the navy?

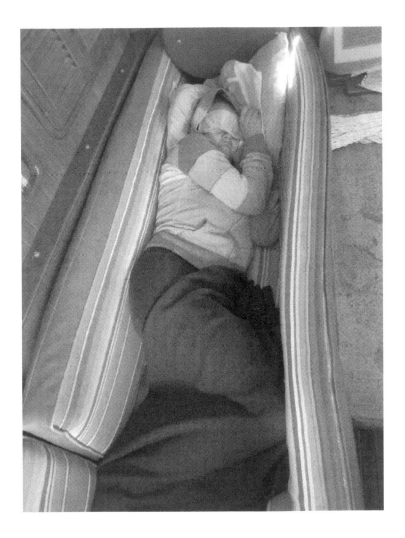

April 8, 2014: Friendship

I never imagined that the mid-ocean could be so calm. No wind, no waves, nothing. Not a ripple disturbs the glassy calm. The foresail is flapping, so we rigged the pole to keep it open and away from the shrouds and lifelines.

I finally fall asleep for my morning nap, when I hear Rick calling.

"Dolphins!" he exclaims excitedly.

They are everywhere, at least twenty of them! These are beautiful dark dolphins with white spots on their backs. I first thought that, as usual, they had come to play in the waves that are generated by the bow. But we are not making a bow wave in our becalmed state. On this occasion, the friendly visitors are busy with something else: hunting.

Dolphins usually swim just underneath the surface at a slow, steady pace. Today, they are diving deep, but I still have a clear view of them because the ocean is so incredibly clear. Their movements are quick and wild. At such moments, I wish I had an underwater camera glued onto the keel, or even a glass hull. Or some kind of inverse periscope so I could observe the action without becoming part of it.

We once had a crew member who showed a haughty disdain when a pod of dolphins approached the boat, claiming he had "seen them before." Apart from the umbrage caused by the rather patronizing insinuation that my enthusiasm stemmed from this being my first contact with dolphins, I was reminded of the old adage that "only boring people get bored." I prayed to Neptune that there would never come a day where my senses were so dulled that the arrival of these wonderful creatures would leave me similarly unimpressed.

When we lived in Mexico, dolphins swam past us several times a day. They often spent hours chasing the little fish hiding underneath our boat. But my favorite show by far was the dance that they perform with pelicans. Well, maybe "dance" is not the most suitable term. Biologists call it "symbiosis": Dolphins chase fish which flee toward the surface, where they are caught by birds which dive on them from above. Their splashes scare the remaining fish and send them back into the path of the dolphins.

This is an incredible performance of jumping, diving, and splashing, but I am not entirely sure if the dolphins really get the best of this deal. Pelicans seem to enjoy stealing fish from the mouths of dolphins way too often for the arrangement to be equitable. When this happens for the first time, the dolphins stand off and pretend not to be interested in the fish anyway, like Aesop's fox with the sour grapes. After the second or third incident, the dolphins abandon this rather aloof attitude and squabbles begin to ensue.

I once saw a pelican with a stolen fish in its beak sit down on the surface of the sea to eat his recently purloined spoils when, from the depths of the ocean, an angry dolphin came shooting toward him gathering speed at a phenomenal rate. There was a clash, a splash, and a loud 'squark' as the pelican became airborne and the fish tumbled back to the sea. I may have imagined it, but the dolphin looked like he was sniggering.

What a pity that there are no pelicans this far out on the ocean to amuse us in our becalmed state.

Just the slightest breath of wind arises, so we try our new toy, a special type of spinnaker called a Parasailor. Designed in Germany, it is an unusual sail with an opening about a third of the way down and a kind of wing (similar to the one used by paragliders) flying forward of that opening. The idea is that in light airs from astern, the wind will not only fill the sail, but a part of that wind will pass through the opening and inflate the paraglider which, in turn, will hold the sail up and stop it flopping about all over the place. It is quite an expensive sail; but just before we left, a cruiser offered it to us for a tenth of the price. We just had to jump at the opportunity.

After rigging all the necessary lines for its deployment, our deck looks like a plate of spaghetti, but there is method in this apparent chaos. We release this bit of high-tech nylon from its sock. What a show! Light wind sails are always beautiful with their bright colors and impressive dimensions, but this one is doubly striking with its lime green wing unfolding and pulling the sail upward. *Calypso* begins to crawl forward like the proverbial painted boat upon a painted sea.

As I sit at the helm watching *Calypso*, I see a friend whom I know well and fully trust. I simply cannot imagine embarking on a journey such as this with a boat I did not trust. If I had any doubts about her ability to take us 3,000 nautical in all conditions, I would surely have had a nervous breakdown by now.

The same applies to the crew. Crossing an ocean with someone you do not trust 100% is a psychological (and sometimes actual) suicide.

At strategic points such as Gibraltar and the Panama Canal, there are always young travelers looking to hitch a ride across the ocean. They would like to experience ocean sailing, but they do not have their own vessel. So, they go looking for someone who needs an extra crewmember on board. Often, both sides are happy with the experience, but this is far from a foregone conclusion. Living on a boat together is challenging and can easily end up in conflict. Even life partners and good friends can find themselves in acrimonious disputes at sea. In such a small space, all the masks are quickly gone, and people eventually show their true nature. The same applies to relationships. Everything that is hidden or suppressed finds corporeal form in very short order. The divorce rate could be halved if every engaged couple spent a few months on a boat at sea before tying the knot.

Even Rick and I have the occasional run-in. Today, whilst looking at the chart, I stated that we should sail as far west as possible, but Rick disagreed. He wanted to go south. It made me angry because I am in charge of navigation. For a whole month, I read, listened, studied, and checked the advice from various sources, so I had my reasons. I think I was angry because I felt he didn't trust my opinion. He pointed out that, being the captain, he is also responsible for my mistakes and that it is his job to verify and question my decisions. I am too stubborn to let it go, so I remain in a cloudy mood. To be fair, I do not even think that fight was about navigation. I suspect that being becalmed is playing on our nerves.

We are moving very slowly. The view on the nautical chart makes us frustrated; we move about one inch per day, and we have at least two feet to go. At this pace, we will need another 52 days. Good thing I bought enough food to feed a whole army of hungry Italians!

So far, we have used very little water, but we also noticed that two jerry cans are empty, which means they are leaking. Bummer.

We are very careful with our water usage, but this morning I pampered myself with a shower – well, if you can call it that – it was more like an elephant being hosed down at the zoo.

We have a saltwater tap on deck, which we normally use to wash the boat down. However, today Rick gave me a wonderful hosing while I was shampooing my hair. Shampoo lathers up much better than soap in salt water, so we do the bulk of our washing like that and reserve the fresh water for the final rinse.

I am not in a rush to get anywhere. I could easily drop these flogging sails and watch movies or read books until we get some more wind. I have begun to like it here on the flat, oily-calm ocean. Fortunately, Rick is a little more pragmatic and is trying to keep the boat moving however slowly. Starting the engine did not even cross our minds. Somehow, it does not fit our sailing ethos.

The autopilot still does not work. If the wind vane breaks down, we're in serious trouble. It is a new unit by a great manufacturer which we fitted ourselves, so I am fairly confident it will go the distance. There is always sheet-to-tiller steering which we were quite happy with for years on our previous boat *Marutji*, and we still have our home-made kit on board *Calypso* if the need arises. So we should be good.

After lunch, two birds visit us. They draw figures-of-eight in the sky, hunting and playing. It is nice to see they have each other. Being in such a remote part of the world is hard enough, but it must be even harder if you are completely alone.

Those solo sailors have some fortitude! I can see that it must be a unique life experience, and I greatly admire anyone who chooses to embark on such a feat, but I still think that man is a very social being and needs to interact with others. If I am completely honest, I admit that sometimes I wish to be alone on the boat. But I know it's not a genuine desire, because it always surfaces when I don't immediately get exactly what I want. For example, when we cannot agree on where we will be anchored or where we will go, I always think:

"One day I will have my own boat and I will go where I want!"

Of course, I say this out of the temporary flash of anger. Single-handing is a demanding job, and I doubt that it would really make me happy. A few little compromises is a small price to pay for having someone to share life's experience with. With Rick by my side, I can share my thoughts, express my fears, ask for advice, get help, or simply cook a romantic dinner for two.

Anyway, single-handers often end up being slightly mad. The first sailor to circumnavigate solo is perhaps the most obvious example. Joshua Slocum wrote about being visited by the (imaginary) pilot from Columbus's ship *Pinta*. The visits became so regular that Slocum began to call him "my old friend".

Everyone needs a friend. Real is best, but imaginary will do.

April 9, 2014: Sluggishness

I am extremely sleepy. *Calypso* is standing still, the sails are flapping, nothing interesting is happening. I watched two movies then the computer ran out of battery. I cannot charge it at night because without solar power we don't have enough capacity. I'll have to wait until morning. I am bored and tired. Unusually, Rick went to sleep in the forepeak, that's how flat the sea is. I take advantage of the empty settee and lie down for a second. I may close my eyes just for a moment. I am worried about sleeping too long, so I set our high-tech alarm (a $3 kitchen timer for boiling eggs) for fifteen minutes. It has a very loud report, and I don't want to wake Rick up. I slip it under my pillow and turn off the light.

A few minutes later, I see a big motorboat just a dozen feet away from our bow. It's moving fast and heading straight for us! How can they not see us? Oh God! We'll crash! In three seconds! Three, two, one ... and I open my eyes. My heart is beating like crazy. The dream was my brain's way of warning me that I had overslept. The pressure of the pillow had turned off the alarm, and I had slept for half an hour. Everything is still silent, except for my heart pounding. I know it was just a nightmare, but I still have to run to the cockpit and make sure there are no boats heading for us. What a relief!

Everything is calm; a slight mist creates a proper pirate movie atmosphere. I need a little time to calm down before

I dare to go below again. I will never again put the alarm under the pillow, I promise!

Suddenly I am very awake, so I may as well have a snack with the leftovers. While on passage, it is really worth making large portions when you cook so you can find a proper, healthy snack without creating any more mess or washing up.

The next time I go to the cockpit, I see a strong light low above the horizon, and I recognize it - that's the star that I was running from a few days ago. This time I am not falling for it, but I am still going out more often to check if everything is fine. Somehow, I cannot accept that it is only a star. It is just too bright. It casts a reflection on the sea every bit as bright as the moon. Then I remember that yesterday I heard on the radio something about a space station orbiting through this area. That must be it.

I leave Rick to sleep until nine as there is really nothing to do and I am awake now.

In the middle of the morning, we try to raise the drifter, the lightest sail we have, but there is simply not enough wind to fill it. I guess we're going to stand still for another day.

I could get angry and pull my hair out, or I can just accept the situation. Buddhism teaches us that suffering is the difference between what we experience and what we would like to experience. If I resist accepting reality as it is, I create my own suffering. If I promise myself again and again that I will be happy when "x" occurs, I am sentencing myself to eternal dissatisfaction. The truth is that if the "x" we are so keenly suspending our happiness for ever does come to pass, it keeps us happy for a mere instant until the human mind finds another "x" that we decide we must have or can't be happy without. We constantly set ourselves new milestones:

"I'll be happy when I buy a new car, when I pay off my debt, when I get married, when I get divorced, when I am rich, when the wind will start to blow ...," an elegantly simple and effective recipe for constant dissatisfaction.

I am slowly learning that I can only be happy if I do not allow external factors to influence my feelings. Of course, there are always things that influence my daily mood, but that basic well-being derived from inner peace depends only on me. Not money, not success, not Rick, and not the wind.

We decided a long time ago never to be in a hurry, so we often find ourselves becalmed. Other boats start the engine; we wait. This training in patience is now paying off. The environmental issues notwithstanding, very few sailboats have enough fuel to cross the entire Pacific Ocean, so it pays to see your fuel as an emergency system and develop a little patience.

I am thinking how western civilizations have forgotten about this art of slowness. Doctors have long warned us that we should take more time for meals instead of gobbling down sandwiches on the go while we hurry from the office to the car. There are already countless books written about the importance of slowing down one's daily pace, so I am not going to beat that particular drum too heavily here. However, I have noticed that even sailors, who were once quite a patient group, are becoming increasingly infected by the speed disease. Yacht racing

71

continues to grab the headlines and public attention at the expense of simple voyaging. If we compare modern boat designs with those of fifty years ago, we find that every year the hulls got thinner, the boats got lighter, the keels narrower, and the masts higher. The goal is to build/own/sail the fastest sailboat, even at the expense of security and seaworthiness.

This is all well and good if you have millions of dollars and can rebuild your boat every few months and generally give these ocean greyhounds all the attention they need. However, most people do not and therefore they need to find sponsors - and this is where the trouble starts. Sponsors are interested in coverage, so the system rewards those who are first past the post and to hell with seaworthiness. Storm techniques successfully used by seafarers for centuries to survive in the worst conditions are now forgotten because they offer no competitive advantage. For many, going sailing for the pleasure of doing so is no longer enough. It seems necessary to always have a goal: to circumnavigate the world, to cross the Atlantic as quickly as possible, to win the local regatta, to set new records. So, when the wind runs out, it seems a natural evolution of mind to turn on the engine and hurry onward because arriving at our destination has become more important than the joy of sailing.

In my teens, I read a quote that really stuck in my memory. The great Slovenian climber Nejc Zaplotnik wrote:

"Whoever seeks the goal will remain empty when he has reached it, but whoever finds the way will always bear the goal within himself."

The essence of sailing should not be to reach the destination, but to enjoy the journey toward it; to use the forces of nature in our favor and to surrender to the wind instead of fighting it (which sometimes means changing the destination), to get lost in the infinite blue and become part of it.

I confess that, in the past, I have also been guilty of this attitude. Focusing on my destination has always left me frustrated, especially when the wind runs out. As I have developed as a sailor though, I have learned to love the journey itself, and speed has become almost irrelevant.

April 10, 2014: Concern

Yesterday, I waxed philosophical about how slow sailing does not bother me at all, but I am not so sure about it anymore. We spent the whole night in the same place waiting for the wind. I had lowered the sails because they were just getting ruined.

In the morning I check the night's progress and the results are confusing. Today our log (which measures the total distance sailed) shows 60 miles less than yesterday. How is this even possible?

The log is a tiny wheel attached to the underwater part of the boat. It rotates when the water runs past it, like a tiny watermill. When we go fast, lots of water passes by and therefore the log rotates faster and counts more nautical miles. When we go slowly, less water passes and less miles are recorded. But, to lose miles from the total, that's really confusing.

I have been thinking about it for some time, and I have an idea. When we stood still last night, the current must have been faster than us. The current is coming from behind us, so perhaps by overtaking us, it made the wheel turn backwards and rewind the miles. Not entirely sure if this is possible, but this is my best guess at the moment.

The log tells us how many miles we have sailed through the water, but our real distance is better measured as distance over ground. Water also moves due to sea currents, so I need to add that speed to our speed. It is like swimming

74

down a river. The speed of my movement would be the sum of the speed of my swimming and the speed of the river.

I grew up on Adriatic Sea where the currents are almost non-existent. Consequently, I never gave them much thought. However, I discovered that in many areas of the world, the story is very different. I learned this the hard way on the very first week of my sailing with Rick in Australia.

We had just finished an overnight passage and had anchored by the town of Ballina about three miles up the eponymous river to escape some boisterous weather. We did not plan to go ashore, so the dinghy was still on deck. After lunch, I was doing the dishes on the swim platform that juts out from the stern of the boat, when I dropped the sponge I was using. I was in my bikini anyway, so without thinking, I jumped straight in after it (I hate rubbish in the sea!). After three big strokes underwater, I surfaced and grabbed the lost sponge. Turning back toward the boat, I thought to myself,

'Wow, those must have been very good underwater strokes, I swam so far!'

Of course, despite my conceit, I had not just morphed into an Olympic swimmer, but was being sucked downstream at an ungodly pace by the current. The true severity of the situation was revealed to me when I tried to swim back to the boat. I wasn't getting any closer. In fact, despite being a fairly strong swimmer, I was still moving away from the boat at quite a clip toward the boisterous river bar and the open ocean beyond.

A few months earlier, I had completed a Lifewatch course so at least I knew what not to do and could clearly hear the instructor's voice repeating the mantra: "Don't panic and don't get exhausted!"

Repeating this to myself helped me to keep things under control. My short and not very interesting life story would probably have ended that very day if Rick had not been in the cockpit and observed me struggling behind the boat.

He threw me a rescue line which landed just a few feet away (very good throw indeed as I was by now a good 40 feet from the boat!). As much as I tried, though, I just did not have the strength to make up even that little bit of ground. My superman of a boyfriend managed to run forward, throw the dinghy off the bow, grab the oars, and launch himself into it in one fluid motion while it was moving quickly downstream. I somehow managed to slow my drift so Rick could catch up with me and haul me aboard, but now we were both in the dinghy being swept downstream toward the turbulent river bar.

Rick managed to turn the dinghy around and lean his back to the oars. While he never ceases to amaze me with his super-human strength, it took nearly all of it to make half a knot back toward our boat. I wondered if perhaps it might be beyond even his endurance. We were spared the opportunity to find out when a local resident came to our aid in a motorboat. This guy had witnessed our dilemma from his cottage on the river bank and, with typical Aussie "have a go" mentality, hopped into his little tinny and rushed to our aide. Suitably chastised, I stepped back aboard *Marutji* still holding on to the sponge, whose rescue had prompted this unplanned adventure, as some kind of consolation prize. I was a little taken aback when Rick, without a word, took it from me and threw it into the sea. That was my lesson: do not die for a sponge.

I have not forgotten this, and current is still the thing I fear most in the sea.

Even when not chasing sponges, I still have to think about tides when I plan our navigation. Often the tide outranks the wind. I know this sounds odd. Even my friends from the sailing club were skeptical when I expressed this view. In the Adriatic, the wind is always the most important factor. But the experience of sailing across Australia and Mexico has convinced me that, as the English say, "tide is king." Let me elaborate with an example.

Take a boat that moves at five knots (which for non-sailors is eight kilometers or five miles per hour).

Without any tide, the 80-mile journey from Ensenada to San Diego would take 16 hours. If the boat leaves at 5 a.m., they will arrive at 9 p.m., just in time for dinner and bed.

Now, let's imagine that there is a strong current flowing up the Californian coast at a speed of three knots which helps them sailing north. Their speed in this case would be eight knots. So they will sail only ten hours and arrive in San Diego at 3 p.m., with plenty of time for a walk around the city and a sunset drink. Favorable currents are great. Whenever we find one, I feel like I have won the lottery. The story is very different with an opposite current. In this case, we need to deduct the current from our speed, so five minus three equals two. That mean the same journey would take an astonishing 40 hours!

As you can see, the current makes a large difference even before we consider the strange wave patterns that form when the wind and current are moving in opposite directions.

Mid-ocean currents are usually not so powerful though. They are also quite predictable and very well described on nautical charts. In our voyage from Mexico to Polynesia, we will have a favorable current most of the way. At least that's something! If the wind fails to appear, the current will take us to Tahiti in time to be issued our pension books.

Typical. After being extremely sleepy during my night watch, I cannot sleep now I have the chance, so tonight I am up and checking our fresh food supplies. I have to examine them at least once a week to throw away whatever is rotten and use whatever is approaching the borders of edible. I know it sounds like a simple job, but with such a mountain of fresh supplies, it takes me at least two hours. Every carrot is individually wrapped in newspaper, which I have to change weekly because of the moisture it traps. I empty the fridge, examine everything, and rearrange the veggies by maturity - the ripest has to be on top of the pile. I cut off any bad bits and peel off any bad leaves from lettuces and cabbages. Tomatoes are the least work because I bought them very strategically. I picked seven different levels of maturity, ranging from soft red to bright green, so they ripen at different times, which is great.

Bananas are a different story altogether. There is no space in the fridge, so they hang in the cabin. I bought green ones, but I still know that they will ripen too fast and, of course, all at the same time. Bananas are evil like that. I keep watching them, and they are green, sour, and hard. Yet I know that the moment I look away for a second, they will immediately ripen and start to rot. Panic! How the hell can we eat 47 bananas in two days? We can't. So, on goes the oven and my "inner baker" goes wild. I make banana cookies, banana muffins, banana bread, banana pancakes, banana smoothies, fried bananas with butter and cinnamon, sliced bananas with chocolate sauce and coconut, and so on. We have bananas coming out of our ears, and I promise myself that I will never buy that many bananas again. After a few weeks of course, I will forget all about it and return from the market with another huge bunch of bananas and a big smile on my face. It is lucky that Rick cares less about food than almost any other subject under the sun, as this allows me to indulge my lack of short-term memory and fetish for bargain bananas without any marital repercussions.

The last job is turning over the potatoes and checking for rotten ones. I unlock and lift the floorboard where they are stored (all our floorboards are locked down in case we are rolled over in a storm. It is quite enough to be upside down and fearing for your life without being pelted with old spuds, Rick's less popular tools, and forgotten laundry). Instead of the usual dusty compartment, I notice water in the bilge the color of something akin to potato soup.

Oops! Not good.

"Chico!" I call Rick. "There is water in the bilge!"

Rick eventually arrives, and the first thing he does is stick a finger in it and pop it in his mouth to taste the water.

"It is salty. Good." He declares with puzzling confidence.

"Good?" I exclaim. "Since when is seawater in a boat a good thing?"

"Well, at least it is not a leak in our freshwater tank."

He is right. Typically English, he seems relieved we can have a cup of tea whilst sinking.

I wipe the bilge dry and fill it with paper towels in order to see where the water is coming from. An hour later I check again, and the towels are soaked. There is more water than I thought! On further investigation, I find a small stream flowing from the bow.

We have to find the leak, which means crawling under the bed in the forepeak cabin. The bedding, the mattress, and everything we have stored there all has to come out. What a joy! We spend the whole afternoon tracing this bloody leak and the general consensus is that it is coming from the bobstay chain plate, which is exactly on the waterline. We never noticed the leak before, possibly because we never had the bow crashing into such big waves before.

I am very concerned, while Rick seems much calmer and decides to turn off the automatic bilge pump and empty the bilge using the manual pump every six hours in order to monitor the amount of water coming in. (What a good idea! I would never have thought of that). For now, the flow is stable, about five liters of water every six hours.

Rick says that every boat leaks at least a little bit and that I should not worry too much about it. I would still be much happier if our bilge was completely dry. As I lie in my berth, I am regaled with nightmarish images of sinking. I know that I have to fall asleep as soon as possible, otherwise I will be too tired to keep a good watch. In these circumstances, only meditation can help me. I focus on my breathing and slowly forget about everything else. The waves rock me like a baby (admittedly a baby with an over-enthusiastic parent), and I slowly drift into the world of dreams.

April 11, 2014: Minimalism

Another very calm day. There is no big swell, and I feel good enough to sit by the chart table and read some emails without getting seasick. I read each message from home with a blend of happiness and melancholy. The single sideband modem is too slow to answer everyone, but I'll reply as soon as we reach land.

A journalist wants to have an interview with me for an article about alternative jobs. She thinks I belong in it. I never considered my writing as a real job, but it is a fact that royalties for my articles are currently my only income. We are not talking big numbers here, but this money helps bring food to the table. We do not make much with writing, but we do not spend much either.

However, I certainly do not feel I lack anything. Sure, there are many things that I have to give up. Some cruisers' blogs are full of dinners at this or that restaurant, exploring every island with a rented car, nights in expensive resorts, or flying to Europe to ski for several months while the boatyard crew takes care of the maintenance.

We cannot afford all of this; but this was our choice, and we wouldn't have it any other way. Sure, we could go back to work and save all our life for a glorious vacation at the end, but life is way too short to behave like that. Especially because we are not giving up important things. We are giving up the superfluous, and somehow, I feel that this is something extremely good.

More emails from home including a detailed weather forecast from a sailing friend. I also learn that the story of *Rebel Heart* is currently the main news in the US media. Apparently, our friends have become scapegoats for the moral majority, and the whole of America is accusing them of irresponsible parenting. I would like to write to them and find out what really happened, but I imagine they have their hands full answering questions from the media, so I'll wait for things to calm down.

After a morning of fitful sleep, I start sewing our new flag. Maritime rules demand that every boat must display the flag of its country of registration from the stern and also the flag of the country where it is currently sailing from the starboard spreader (about halfway up the mast). *Calypso* sails under the English ensign, which has been slightly torn in the Mexican wind, so I patch it up. Then I dig out the French flag, which we will need when we arrive at the Marquesas.

I need to add a string to attach it to the boat. Of course, if I had bought a real nautical flag from a marine chandlery, the string would already be attached, but the addition of the word 'nautical' would have immediately quadrupled the price. Yacht chandleries are very expensive, and, in most cases, an identical product can be found in the local hardware store for a lot less. Flags cost about $20 in a chandlery. On our voyage across the Pacific, we'll need at least nine of them, so to save some money I ordered them online from a website for football fans for one dollar each. Admittedly, the quality is not as good as the "nautical" ones, but how often do you really need them? Once in a lifetime for most people. Anyway, they all fly off at some point, regardless of price. By adding the string myself, I saved more than a hundred dollars, which is not a bad payment for two hours of sewing.

I am making pasta with zucchini and bacon for lunch. As always, I put a mixture of fresh and seawater on to boil. I consider it a little silly to add salt to precious fresh water while having a limitless supply of salt water around us. With trial and error, I have found that about one third seawater is optimum for pasta.

Today, I also checked how much fresh water we have used so far. It is hard to measure the exact amount, but a good guess is 45 liters, i.e., about four liters (slightly more than a US gallon) a day. This is great news. Fresh water is the most precious thing aboard. We can survive without pretty much everything else except drinkable water. We have always been very careful about conserving it, but on this passage, we are even more extreme. You can't be too careful! We pretty much only use it for drinking and cleaning our teeth. We wash in seawater, and after that I usually rinse my face, but that's it. I have learned not to be bothered by salty hair or skin.

Anyway, we are approaching the doldrums, the area near the equator known for its downpours and lack of wind. We will be able to collect some rainwater and have a good wash. *Calypso* could also use a decent shower.

April 12, 2014: Panic

Some people say that sailing is endless boredom interrupted by moments of complete terror. Today I certainly agree with this statement.

I have started to feel the lack of sleep. In the morning, I am in a terrible mood, crowned by a killer headache. I take an aspirin and hope to finally get some decent rest. Suddenly, a new sound interrupts the deep silence. I raise my ears and I soon realize what it is: The wind generator is turning! We finally have some wind!

We immediately raise the mainsail and start sailing south again. Yippee! I laugh and jump around like a playful child. It is unbelievable how happy the wind can make me these days. Other times, I find myself scared, angry, or frustrated by it. In fact, the wind is responsible for almost all of the emotions I experience out here.

We sail under Parasailor all day and make good progress. This sail is a godsend, but if things go wrong (and they do!), it can become dangerous. Any spinnaker is hard enough to deal with in the daylight, let alone at night, so we always do the wise thing and take it down before dark. It should be an easy job, but today, the snuffer (which is supposed to slip down the sail to push the wind out of it) is stuck at the top. Pulling and bashing the lines does not help. We have to drop the sail without it.

While lowering the sail at the mast, I keep an eye on Rick, who is collecting it on the foredeck. For just a second, I take my eyes off him to look at the halyard in my hand, and I make a big mistake - I drop the sail faster than he can collect it. Just then a large wave tilts the boat forward, the bowsprit goes underwater and takes the sail with it. In a second, the Parasailor is under the keel and streaming out toward the stern. Rick can hardly hold it. The lines of the wing got tangled up around his arm and are dragging him toward the water.

The panic completely fogs my brain, and I have absolutely no idea what to do. Should I stop the boat? Should I grab hold of Rick? Or should I run around in all directions at once, wildly flapping my arms in the air?

Seeing that I am clearly erring toward the flappy option, Rick calls out, "Unclip the halyard!"

Of course! I grab the sock, open the halyard clip, and throw the top of the sail in the water. Instead of acting like a giant water catcher slowly dragging my partner over the side, it now streams out like a flag in the sea and has lost its power sufficiently to the point where Rick and I can haul it on deck. I do not even check the damage as I am still shaking with fear.

Rick makes me some of the posh hot mint chocolate we bought in the US to help me calm down. He is smiling, but I am silently telling myself off for a stupid mistake that would have dampened his smile a bit!

It is interesting how differently our brains work when we are in panic mode.

As a teenager in Italy, I would go caving on the weekends with my friends. At the time, a new piece of gear was being tested that allowed the caver to control his descent by squeezing a handle that reduced friction on the rope. The harder you squeezed, the quicker you descended. All that was required to stop the descent was to release the handle. It was a total flop. As soon as a caver found himself descending too quickly, his natural reaction was to squeeze harder, which would speed up his descent and cause him to squeeze even harder. And so on. Even though they knew they had to ease their hold, in the heat of the moment, many cavers could simply not bring themselves to do it. They were still squeezing. I am aware that this sounds ridiculous, and it may be hard to imagine how anyone could be quite so stupid. But a real emergency changes our thought parameters, and, until you have been there, it is far too easy to criticize.

I wonder what I can do to improve my panic mode. My guess is that only hands-on experience really works. Reading books, studying, and drill are valuable activities. But the ways a sailing boat can fail are so myriad, it is near impossible to prepare for every eventuality. Only by gathering many experiences and becoming accustomed to thinking creatively under stress can we really prepare ourselves for the most demanding situations.

April 13, 2014: Fear

Finally, it is warm enough to dispose of clothes. The sun is shining, and the wind is blowing steadily.

I have been putting it off but, finally, I get the recently keelhauled Parasailor out of its bag for inspection. I find twelve holes, but luckily, they are all small. The sail is salvageable. I spend the morning patching it up with sail tape, then I stow it back in the bag. I'll let it rest for a few days. It is definitely tired. I know we are.

At around noon, I remember that today is Easter. My family will be sitting around the table, admiring the blossoming almond trees in our garden and eating the traditional "potica" cake and excellent baked ham with horseradish. Oh, how happily I would swap my current bowl of fish and rice for a hearty Slovenian Easter breakfast!

Toward the end of my watch, the wind picks up even more, and I start to feel a sense of foreboding. I am not sure exactly why. Fears can sometimes be difficult to isolate. Yesterday's events with the Parasailor reminded me of how very alone we are out here. If anything happens, no one can help us. If Rick had fallen into the water yesterday, if the heavy sail had dragged him under the water ... I don't even want to think about it!

There are some other boats in the area, but the closest is 400 miles away. It would be easier if we had a boat behind us, but in this group, we are the last one. Those who left after us are at least a week behind.

I once read a book about a couple who found themselves sailing in a cyclone. In the middle of the night, a big wave rolled the boat over. He was at the helm while she was in the saloon. She hit her head on the table and lost consciousness. When she woke up, the cyclone was gone and so was her boyfriend. The sea took him. The boat was a wreck, without mast or sails, without the engine or electronics. After the initial few days of despair, this brave woman rolled up her sleeves, set a jury rig (makeshift mast and sail), and sailed on. She was obviously a great navigator, as she managed to sail to Hawaii where she got the medical attention she needed. This is a true story. I read it in three days and cried for most of it. Through those tears I discovered my biggest fear: that Rick would fall overboard.

We often speak about it and agree that this is a serious danger indeed. That's why we decided long ago that neither of us will ever leave the cockpit while the other is asleep. If there is no other way to solve a problem, then I wake him up and tell him that I have to go forward. As soon as I return, I shout, "I am back!" and he can fall back asleep again. Of course, he does the same on his watch. I am much happier knowing that he will never be on deck while I am asleep.

We always wear a life jacket, but we are no less careful because of that. It is almost impossible to find a person in the ocean, life jacket or not, and we know it. A small head gets lost in a large swell very quickly.

Obviously, the best course of action is to stay on board, and all efforts should be directed toward this end. When we walk on a sailing boat, we should be acting as if it were the edge of a cliff. We sailors should have the same safety attitude as mountaineers when we move around our decks in a seaway because the repercussions of falling are pretty much the same. So we should always have three points of contact and use a safety tether. In stormy weather, we are tethered even when sitting in the cockpit. You just cannot be too careful.

I have noticed that a healthy fear of falling overboard has become second nature to me now. When the wind picks up and the waves grow, my grip changes automatically. I feel how my hand squeezes the handrail more firmly, every step is more tentative, and every planned action is considered more deeply.

I confess to being slightly annoyed when I see sailing couples where the husband doesn't care to teach his wife (or she does not care to learn) the most basic skills for living aboard and sailing safely. To me, this seems inconceivable and irresponsible, but I know some women who live on boats and sail around the world without actually knowing how to control their vessel. They can follow orders fairly well, which makes them at least good crew, but without leadership, they would not be able to reef the sails, gybe safely, or stop the boat.

Famous female sailors like Ellen McArthur, Naomi James, Dee Caffari, Jessica Watson, Laura Dekker, Pippa Wilson, and many others are living proof that, in sailing, gender is not important, so this is even less excusable today than it was twenty years ago.

I once attended a "Women Who Sail" conference on the lovely roof terrace of the yacht club in La Cruz, Mexico. Upwards of forty sailing women attended, and many of them complained that their husband could not, or would not, take the time to teach them about the boat. While this is no real excuse (not all sailors make good instructors and the husband is not the only source of sailing information), it does highlight a serious issue that negatively impacts the efficiency and enjoyment of many sailing women.

These taciturn husbands would do well to remember the wise words of Cape Horn sailor Peter Cookingham who is one of the best sailors I know:

Teach your spouse everything you know and be nice to her because, not only should she be able to pick you up if you fall overboard, she will have to want to as well!

April 14, 2014: Wake

Today we are celebrating the 1,000 miles mark. There are still another 2,000 to go. This Pacific Ocean is bigger than I thought.

Rick is lying on the saloon berth with headphones in his ears, looking at the ceiling, mumbling in French. I admire his discipline in learning new languages, well actually, in everything. I always give up too soon. I tried to learn English a dozen times without success until I did the only thing that works for me: I moved to an English- speaking country all by myself. If I wanted to order a coffee, find a street, or a place to stay, I simply had to learn how to say it. And I did. Rick helped me a lot with it. I still remember reading him *Swallows and Amazons* in the evenings, stopping when I found a word I did not know.

Last night, a bird joined us and is currently resting on the bowsprit. If I am not mistaken, it is a brown booby. Rick says we should name it. I get the feeling he is already emotionally attached to it. Yesterday I saw him bringing the bird some water and a flying fish for a snack.

Flying fish! Every morning I have to collect all these unfortunate creatures that had their planned re-entry into the sea interrupted by our deck. If I miss one hiding in the dorade vent or under the dinghy, its aroma will let me know sooner or later.

Today I saw a whole school of them flying over the whitecaps. There were more than 200 fish skimming the water, their green wings unfolding over their flashing silver bodies like marine dragonflies.

The other big event of the morning was Rick discovering a scented purple liquid that flooded the locker under the sink. A one-gallon plastic container of detergent had burst. My fault for trying to save two dollars by doing the shopping in a cheap warehouse. Anyway, I don't really care. At least the boat smells nice.

The waves are getting bigger. Now they are over ten feet high and occasionally a monster dumps itself in the cockpit. Rick's newly acquired hatred of being drowned in bed means we keep the companionway door permanently closed, so this time we are ready.

I am sitting in the cockpit looking aft, watching our wake. A white sparkling trail between big waves - that's all that remains behind us. And even this trail will disappear very soon, in a minute or two, three at most. Nobody will ever know that we passed this way.

A journey through the sea does not leave any trace.

Something like that is not possible on land. When we walk on a path in the forest, we leave footprints. When we climb in the high mountains, we make the rocks smoother, although we do not notice it. Even motor vehicles leave a footprint - if only an environmental one. The same goes for motorboats.

I derive a great deal of satisfaction from knowing that my trip is environmentally friendly. I also like the idea that no one will ever repeat exactly the same path. This trail is ours alone and is disappearing behind us. We send a position report once a day, but one minute later we are somewhere else. Apart from that brief moment of certainty, nobody knows where we are.

Nowadays, this is a real luxury.

April 15, 2014: Here and now

On my night watch, I notice the genoa furling line is stuck. It is not really an emergency as there are no squalls around, so I am not going to wake Rick up. But as soon as his sleepy face pokes through the companionway, I go forward to deal with it, safely tethered of course.

Our resident bird, (now named 'Jeff' for some archaic cockney rhyming slang reason that I don't really understand) does not take flight when I move closer to his den on the pulpit, although he keeps a wary eye on my progress.

I was looking forward to my morning nap, but now I lie here and cannot sleep at all. My lower back hurts. I am shifting and turning, but it does not help. I am not just tired and in pain now but frustrated as well. I take some painkillers and turn on the TV. On this passage the big screen we bought a few weeks ago is priceless. Do not get me wrong; I do enjoy being on the ocean, but sometimes I really need a break from it. Especially in bad weather! With a movie, I can fly away and for a moment forget where I am. It is a well-needed rest for my nerves.

Just before lunch, the painkillers finally grab. I am almost asleep when I smell something burning. Rick is just preparing his lunch, so I mutter, "Sweetie, something is burning ..."

He checks the pots and the stove and says everything is fine. Then I open my eyes and I see ... smoke! Something is burning, but not in the galley! The smoke is coming from an electric socket! I jump up and immediately turn off the main power supply. We soon find out that the problem is the little inverter for my computer. I'll not use it again - a fire is the last thing we need out here.

I lie down again and try to calm my beating heart. A few long deep breaths, and I am finally asleep... but not for long! A call from the cockpit wakes me up just a few minutes later.

"Jasna, come! We caught a fish!"

I forget about sleeping and stumble out into the cockpit. Rick is already reeling the line in. I grab a net to bring the fish aboard (we just cannot bring ourselves to use a gaff) and, after a brief struggle, we land a decent-sized Spanish mackerel. Rick cleans the fish in the cockpit while I pack the fresh fillets into the fridge. As soon as we are done, we lay the lines out again and almost immediately we get another bite. This time an even bigger Spanish mackerel! That's going to be enough for at least five meals, so we decide not to send the lure out again. We certainly do not want to catch fish we cannot eat. Even so, we always feel bad about fishing. We are both on the edge of being vegetarians and, although we like eating fish, every time we land one we feel like we must apologize and explain:

"I am sorry that you have to die, little creature, but we are running out of fresh food."

Sometimes we look at each other with sad eyes and make a silent promise not to fish for a while. Rick usually adds:

"What is wrong with lentils anyway?!"

I have given up on my morning sleep, so I turn on the computer and check the email via HF radio. My friend Petra sent a report from home: she has bought an RV and the whole family drove to the coast to look at the sea. She reminds me of how often I went to the sea just to look at it. How many hours I spent sitting on the beach staring into the distance.

I know that one day I will be there again, looking at the horizon from the safety of dry land. I am pretty sure I will nostalgically remember sailing across the ocean. Maybe I'll even want to be here again. So I remind myself that I have to try and savor all the nuances of this experience. Enjoy every day, every hour. Even when I am scared or bored. I have to embrace all the feelings that the day brings, because, otherwise, one day I'll be very sorry that I didn't.

Sometimes we look nostalgically at our past, sometimes we are worried about the future, or dream of a perfect tomorrow. And between the safety of nostalgia and dreams of the future, we forget to notice the present - this very moment. I am sleepy and tired, but hey, I am also in the middle of the freaking Pacific Ocean on a tiny sailboat! How cool is that?!

We are not changing sails that regularly anymore. The wind comes and goes and then it comes and goes again. To act upon every little change is just too tiring. It is not a big deal if we lose half a knot anyway - we will simply arrive at the destination a few days later. This approach is working well. We are not tired; we do not suffer from lack of sleep; we are not irritable; and we make good decisions in a courteous manner.

The evening net brings some friendly voices. I have a quick chat with the schooner *Destiny* which is anchored on the Mexican coast about 1,200 nautical miles away. We met the crew of *Destiny* last year when I was writing an article on unusual sailboats. Their huge wooden schooner is the center of attention in every anchorage and an obvious target for me, so I rowed over to have a look at their floating palace. Over time, we became friends. Now *Destiny* is heading for Costa Rica while we are sailing toward the South Seas. We said our goodbyes over the radio waves, knowing that we would probably never see each other again. You have to accept that when you live on the sea. We constantly make new friends, but soon we are all sailing away, each boat following her own path. I know that's how it must be, but one cannot help being a little sad every time a new friend disappears over the horizon.

I was surprised to hear them so loud and clear over such a long distance – as if they were merely down the road rather than half an ocean away. Sometimes I complain about the cranky, clunky nature of this wartime technology, but a good single sideband radio is actually worth its weight in gold, which, coincidentally, is about what they cost.

As night draws in, we sit in the cockpit and watch a lunar eclipse. Here in the middle of the ocean, we are as far from civilization as it is possible to get without leaving the planet. There are no city lights to steal the darkness, no noise whatsoever, and the magic of the silence is pure and deep. I lie in Rick's arms, staring at the sky and thinking of how full of wonders is our universe.

What a beautiful day! I really did not think it could be improved upon, but I surprised myself by doing just that with an enormous stack of pancakes for breakfast. Only 78 eggs left of the initial 94. I wonder if they will survive until French Polynesia. I have never kept them for so long, but apparently it is possible. When we had no fridge, I learned how to keep them from spoiling, which came in very handy for this passage (there was no space in the fridge whatsoever). First option is to individually coat each egg with Vaseline, which works well. Later, though, I discovered that turning them over twice a week works just as well, and it saves a lot of messiness.

When putting together the shopping list, I followed the example of the great American sailor Lin Pardey who has been crossing oceans all her life. According to her, I should have bought 200 eggs. I decide that half that was more than enough, and to be fair, I still think I bought too many. The hardest thing was to find good storage for them, where they can be safe even in the worst storm. At the end, I put them in a wide drawer and covered them with towels.

Many landlubbers often laugh at me when I go on about the care of eggs. I always get a little offended. These people have no idea that eggs at sea are a devastatingly serious matter.

The news of the day is that Jeff has got a girlfriend. Both birds are now reclining amidships in the lee of the upturned dinghy. They spent all morning having a lovers' tiff, while Rick tried his best at marriage guidance counseling.

"Come on, guys ... there is no need for this..."

They simply ignored him and continued to bicker like politicians.

We are getting closer to the doldrums, the equatorial belt famous for the absence of wind and sudden, violent squalls. Although our destination lies to the southwest, tomorrow we will turn due south in order to reduce the amount of distance we have to cover in this uncomfortable belt. This is more or less where *Rebel Heart* sank. We have this nightmare of running into some of their gear. I really hope we do not.

All day long, I am concerned with the question of when to turn south. The boats ahead of us report bad weather with strong winds and huge waves, so I am tempted to continue west to avoid it. I am afraid that by dragging my heels, we may end up too far west, which could mean having to sail into the wind. We can certainly live without that. Sooner or later, we'll have to sail straight into this nasty weather. But choosing the right moment can spare us the worst of it. I finally decide to ask for help.

I turn on the computer and write a message to Mike, an American sailor and sail maker, who has been an amateur weather forecaster for many years. He studies the weather over the Pacific Ocean constantly, so is probably the best person to ask. I hope he will write back soon.

During the night watch, I am visited by dolphins. There are at least fifteen of them and they stay with us almost all night. Maybe they know I need a distraction from my worries. They play, jump, and dive, which in bioluminescence looks even more fascinating than in daylight. Thank you, dolphins, for a delightful performance.

I check my email early and get the letter I was hoping for. Mike writes:

"The more you sail to the west, the worse it gets. I advise you to turn south right away. If you have already crossed the 125th meridian, I suggest you sail toward the southeast."

Southeast? Away from our destination!?

Despite our reservations, we decide to follow Mike's advice. Rick goes out to the boomkin and sets the wind vane to steer us toward the southeast. I am anxious. Are we sailing straight into hell? What is waiting for us? Rather than stew in our own fear, we get busy by preparing the boat for foul weather. The storms are just a matter of time. I am not really sure what to expect, but I have heard stories of sixty-knot squalls, which are certainly not something to underestimate. Anything loose has to be lashed down or stored below. The shower stall is jammed full of things that normally live outside - cushions, fishing rods, covers, jerrycans.

If there is any lightning in the storm, we could lose all of our electronics, so we have an emergency hand-held GPS safely packed in a metal box as well as an old-fashioned sextant should the worst come to the worst.

Thunderstorms scare me more than anything at sea, because we are totally helpless. If the wind intensifies, we can reef the sails; if the waves grow and start to break, we can heave-to. But, if we are surrounded by lightning, there is absolutely nothing to do but sit and wait.

If someone had asked me a few years ago about the likelihood of being struck by lightning, I would have dismissed it out of hand, probably with a little laugh. But since then, I have met so many sailors who have been hit that I have long since stopped laughing. Some boats were hit in the middle of the sea, others while at anchor in a bay. Some in a marina, and some even in the boatyard.

Therefore, the first lesson is that nowhere is completely safe from lightning, and no prevention system is really effective. If a thunderbolt strikes the boat directly, nothing will stop it. Once we accept this, we can begin to think about how to reduce damage in the event of a strike. Disconnecting all the electronics is always a good place to start. We usually wrap them in aluminum foil and stack them in the oven (which acts like a Faraday cage). This considerably reduces the chances of damage. It is also important that the boat is well grounded. The lightning usually descends down the mast and then searches for a path to the water. With good grounding, much of this energy can be dissipated and maybe the more important parts of the boat spared. Of course, the most important thing is to avoid personal contact with metal surfaces, especially the mast and the standing rigging.

I remember a well-seasoned American sailing duo on a tough-looking Tahiti ketch saying that their preferred method of coping with lightning was to wrap bacon around the base of the mast.

"If we get hit, the bacon is not going to help, but at least it is going to smell divine."

Since I am writing about electronics, let me add that today the autopilot miraculously came back to life. Well, it was not a miracle, it was Rick who for 16 days was taking care of it very diligently: he washed it with acetone, put it out in the sun every morning and back down below every evening (and gave it a few kisses at lunch time). Finally, the device stopped resisting his attentions, and now it works again! This is going to be very handy if we have to motor at any point. A wind vane cannot steer if there is no wind.

The birds are happily pooping all over the boat. The latest stowaway likes to be on the boom and poop on our brand-new precious mainsail, while Jeff seems to be more comfy on the radar, dropping his little gifts on to our best solar panel. I was planning to send them back to the bowsprit, but Rick stood up for them:

"Poor souls! They are lost, and we are their only hope."

He looks at me with those charming, begging eyes and I go soft. Well, I suppose I can keep washing guano off the boat every morning. I have nothing better to do anyway.

Today we are exactly half way but decide to postpone the celebrations for a few days until we get to the equator and leave the storms behind us.

April 18, 2014: Giggling

In the morning, we get our first big squall. Sails disappear in the record time of twenty seconds (we were sooo ready!). The squall brings thirty-knot gusts and a heavy downpour. Our first reaction is to hide down below, until we realize that we were dreaming about this abundance of fresh water for the last three weeks. So off with the clothes and, with soap in hand, we return to the deck. Of course, we shut the companionway behind us to keep the cabin dry.

What followed has to be the most enjoyable shower we've ever experienced. What a great feeling! This must be the definition of joy. We soap each other, sing, and laugh like we do not have a care in the world. The squall eventually calms down and the sun pops out to dry our naked bodies. We had forgotten to bring a towel, so we have to drip dry. It does not take long.

We watch the rain disappear into the distance. No more squalls around for now, so it is time to open the boat up.

But ... hey! The door is locked! From the inside!

How did this possibly happen? Rick knows straight away: last year he installed a dead bolt so that we can lock the companionway from the inside during rough weather. It must have slid into place during a big roll to starboard. We are locked out! Naked! With not even a handkerchief to cover ourselves. The scene is quite hilarious really. I can already see the rescuers laughing at the distressed sailors au naturel.

After having a good laugh at our own stupidity, we start looking into possible solutions. All the hatches have been prudently closed against the squall. The storm boards in the companionway cannot be opened from the outside (we made them so well from a half-inch-thick plexiglass so nobody could break in, not even us). Our only option is to empty the cockpit locker and crawl over the engine. The good news is that, if I can do that, I can probably slide open a small door into the back of the aft quarter berth. The bad news is that the quarter berth is completely packed with spare sails. From that extremely uncomfortable position (spread across the engine), I would have to push three large sails out of the quarter berth and into the saloon.

Rick is too big to climb through that hole, and I am not sure I am strong enough to push all that weight out ... hmmm.

Just as we are discussing the problem, a big wave rolls the boat to port. Rick jumps at the opportunity and kicks the hatch at the right moment. The dead bolt slides back the other way, and the hatch opens. We are saved the embarrassment of being discovered naked and dead from starvation in our own cockpit! I knew this was going to be a good day.

The squalls carry on all day. Every time there is the threat of a squall, we lower all the sails. Since the first big squall, this has turned out to be merely a precaution as the gusts rarely reach more than 25 knots. But why provoke destiny? Better to lose a few miles than lose a few sails out here. After dropping the sails, we usually go down below, lie on the saloon berth, and watch an episode of some escapist TV drama that most definitely does not contain any reference to the sea. The wind cannot do any damage if all the sails are down, so we do not need to worry. The squall arrives; the rain comes down in buckets; the wind screams through the rigging for half an hour; then everything is silent again. By the end of the episode, the squall is over, and we can sail on.

At the end of the day, we're totally exhausted. I regret not keeping track of how many times we raised and lowered the sails.

The advantage of all this rain is that we are suddenly very clean. Before we showered once a week; now we do it three times a day. My skin is singing in gratitude, and my hair is finally free of salty crystals.

My relationship with rain has changed dramatically since I moved aboard a boat. On land, I would run outside at the first drops of rain to scoop up the hanging laundry. Living on a boat, I do the opposite. When I see the black clouds, I start hanging the laundry out. On a boat, fresh water is so valuable that we have a hierarchy for its use: drinking and cooking are the most important, followed by washing. We always wash the dishes in seawater. Rinsing the washing up with fresh water is only worth considering if we are not too far from civilization. That leaves laundry right at the bottom of the list. No sailor is worried if his clothes are a little salty and wrinkled while at sea. While cruising closer to shore, I usually try to wash clothes when I find a river or a convenient tap on land. At sea, though, a tropical downpour is one's best bet. When I see it coming, I festoon every bit of available rigging on *Calypso* with towels, shorts, and t-shirts. Sometimes even bedding. And after a few hours, my laundry is washed and dried under the tropical sun. A simple washing machine.

If the rain is really strong, we place a few jugs and plastic containers on deck - every drop is precious. In one hour of downpour, we can easily collect ten gallons of water. One day of intense rain means we can fill our tanks from the water that lands on our bimini and is cleverly directed below via a hose and simple skin fitting. We can then shower as much as we want! On a rainy day, I love to sit in the cockpit, staring at the jugs filling with what I call 'free water.' I stare at the little stream, almost hypnotized by this miracle, as the most precious thing on earth literally falls out of the sky for free.

The night is the time when I am most worried about squalls. In the dark, it is impossible to see them approaching. The radar can help, so today I am learning to follow their arrival on the screen. Rain shows up like a group of small dots, so I can always see where it is and in which direction it is moving.

I have just noticed that the birds have left us, probably before the squall. What a shame. We'll miss them.

Everyone on the evening radio net complains about severe storms. We are a day or two behind the others, and I hope that the bad weather will pass before we get there. After the net, we download the weather forecast grib file (a low data forecast that can be received via the incredibly slow speeds of HF radio) which clearly shows a big black patch approaching our area. Black means rain, which is usually not good, but there is no way of telling from the grib if there is any lightning or strong wind involved. Anyhow, it docs not look good.

As with all weather forecasts, the time on the file is given in UTC or Greenwich Mean Time rather than local time. I quickly calculate that, on our current course, this storm should be with us in thirty hours. I am trying to determine whether we have enough time to avoid it by sailing south. I study the chart and the grib file for some time, but I feel that something is missing. Finally, I realize that I have made a big mistake in my calculations. For me, April the 19th is tomorrow, but in Greenwich it is today! I was wrong by one whole day! This means that the ugly big depression will arrive in less than six hours and will hit us head on!

We both agree that we do not want to be where we are. But there is no wind. Therefore, for the first time on this trip, we decide to start the engine. If we motor due south, we might be able to avoid the worst weather. In bed, I cannot find peace for a long time. How could I have made such a stupid mistake?

Finally, I get too tired for further recriminations, and I fall asleep.

Rick wakes me at four in the morning, all smiley and jumpy. He enthusiastically explains how he has been sailing the squalls for the last few hours and how much fun it was "sling-shotting" off the back of them.

"I turned off the engine, because we moved faster under sail once I got the hang of it!"

He goes to bed and leaves me on watch. I make myself a cup of tea, grab a few cookies from the "snack cupboard," and head to the cockpit. There are thousands of stars in the sky. The wind is stable, and it looks like we will be able to skirt the edge of this storm. I predict a very easy watch and feel my stress levels return to standby mode. I settle into my comfy watch seat and open a new book, which turns out to be so gripping that I am not even tempted to have a nap. That's good. It would be a shame to miss such a wonderful night.

April 19, 2014: Health

My night watch always ends at eight in the morning. When we left Mexico, the dawn broke at about five, but as we headed west, the dawn started arriving later. Subsequently, my watches are getting darker and darker. Today, for example, first light broke at seven.

The dawn always makes me happy. Maybe I really like daylight, or maybe it is because the dawn signals the end of my watch and I know that I can soon go to sleep. Filled with new energy, I find it easy to do all the tasks that the sunrise requires. First, I need to move the solar panels to the eastern rail and tilt them at an angle so that we can soon get as much sunlight as possible. Then it is time to fish - I take the lure and the line from the pocket on the stern and drop them into the sea. After that, it is time for the sails. In the squally night, Rick set only the staysail. But now the wind is steadily blowing from the south, so I unfurl the genoa as well. I will raise the mainsail as soon as Rick wakes up. I am not supposed to go on deck, and I do not want to wake him up just for that. We will only lose a mile or so by waiting an hour.

At half past eight, I admire a bloody red sunrise amongst dark black clouds. Rick misses so much by always being off watch during sunrise. I get a unique performance every day.

One of the most frequent questions I get from non-sailors is about medical issues. How do we keep healthy? What if something happens in the middle of the sea? And so on. Firstly, I like to point out how living on a boat is much healthier than living on land. The air here is clean; the pace of life is slow; and the food is generally much healthier. When I was a teacher, I used to be constantly ill. Fortunately, fish do not sneeze in my face as often as schoolchildren do. Of course, the lack of a hospital nearby can be a problem, but it is also very rare that we are so far from land.

In addition, we certainly do not set sail on long passages if we are not both 100% fit. Still, offshore, one has to be extremely careful. Accidents can and will happen, and it is good to be ready with an extensive first aid kit and know how to use it. I appreciate that it may sound odd, but the main physical problem we encounter at sea is lack of activity. Passage making can be as sedentary as working in an office. At anchor, we go for long swims or walks, sometimes we play volleyball on the beach, or rent a bike. On passage, though, we have less options as the need to move slowly in a minimal way is a matter of safety.

So far, we have had no problems, but today I am getting a few cramps in my stomach, which I assume is because I haven't been moving much. I haven't been moving at all, now that I think about it: I spend twelve hours per day sitting or strapped into the cockpit or at the chart table. The rest of the time I lie in my bunk, sleeping, reading, or watching a movie.

I am afraid that the pain will only get worse, so in the afternoon I get off my butt and dedicate one hour to gymnastics. I start with several minutes of running on the side deck. It is not the most elegant run because I actually have to hold myself on with both hands to avoid flying into the drink. After getting my heart pumping, I do half an hour of stretching exercises, especially for the lower back, which is my weak point. I mainly do pilates, which are exercises based on maintaining balance and keeping constant control of the body. The boat is doing what it can to throw me off the very balance that I seek to acquire and is therefore giving me a rather unplanned extra workout. I know that I should do this every day, but to be honest, I often just cannot be bothered. Although I am not actually doing much, I am still tired most of the time - such is life on a bouncy boat - and being thrown all over the place while trying to exercise is not very pleasant.

While stretching my neck on the foredeck, I think about this crazy idea of crossing this enormous ocean, this great blue desert that covers half the globe, with only the help of three bedsheets on a stick and the knowledge of how to manage them. The more I think, the more I realize that it is not an easy task at all. Not everyone knows how to do it. There are many sailors in the world, but only a tiny fraction of them ever venture across an ocean. This realization makes me proud of our skills and our courage, and I risk a little further stretch to pat myself on the back.

April 20, 2014: Treasures

If I had no calendar or was not counting the days and miles as required by the demands of prudent navigation, then I would have guessed that today we were getting toward the end of the journey. It really feels like we've been out here for a month already - but the calendar, unaffected by wishful thinking, disagrees. We have been sailing less than three weeks and a look at the chart shows that we are only about halfway.

A month on the ocean is a really long time.

Today we are both very tired. The squalls of the past few days have been psychologically and physically exhausting, so we are taking it easy, just trying to get as much sleep as we can. Probably this will be one of those days when we spend the least time together.

In the last four years, we've been literally inseparable. The only place on the boat where either of us could be really alone is the head (the toilet). As that is not really a pleasant place to be, we have learned to find our own space even if we are together, either in a book or with the headphones on. But it is rare that we are out of one another's field of vision for too long. This passage is very different. When I am asleep, Rick is awake. When I am awake, he sleeps. We see each other only a few hours per day when changing watches, usually when one of us is exhausted and the other still half asleep.

Today, His Holiness King Neptune kindly sent some perfect wind and calm seas our way, so we have not touched the sails since sunrise. The black clouds are finally gone, and it is getting extremely hot. There is no way we can fall asleep without a fan on or a hatch open.

In the middle of the day, whilst doing my usual horizon check, I see something yellow in the water. How exciting! I call Rick, and we are both guessing what it could be. It looks like a buoy, but it is not big enough to be one of those weather stations that you sometimes find in the middle of the ocean. Rick takes over the helm while I crawl up on the bowsprit with a net in hand, ready to catch the mysterious prey. Rick sails close to the little yellow float, and I can easily catch it and bring it aboard. We feel as if we just found the biggest treasure! We make up stories about the history of it, where it came from, how long it had been floating around. The yellow float will probably come in handy sooner or later, but that's not why we are so excited. We are simply happy because something interesting happened. Something that makes this day different from all the others.

I recall sitting around a table with a group of sailors and talking about various objects we found floating in the middle of the sea. There were many balls, buoys, and fenders, but also some much weirder things. The prize for the strangest find was given to Katrin, a lovely Estonian lady who, in the middle of the ocean, found an enormous round pink fender.

"When I lifted it out of the water, I saw that it was almost completely covered with long tusks of seaweed, which gave it a really scary look. Then I spotted the inscription on the top with the name of the boat to which it belonged... "BLACK PEARL!"

A true pirate treasure!

Our find was much less theatrical, but still precious.

A few hours later, I get another surprise. The bait on the fishing line is gone! Since the culprit had bitten off the metal leader wire, there is no big mystery here about the type of fish that did it. We had probably caught a tuna or a dorado, but a shark stole it from us before we even noticed that we had dinner on a string.

Another stormy night. I use the radar to monitor all the squalls and notice that most of them pass by without becoming a danger to us. Only the ones coming from the east sometimes catch us. Every squall brings strong winds, so it is important to closely monitor their direction and speed. When the black clouds are two miles away and moving toward us, it is time for action.

The first major squall of the day arrives at four in the morning. I have no choice but to wake Rick up.

"What is going on?"

"Nothing serious, but we have to reef the sails. A squall is coming. It is two miles away, moving fast, and will be here in less than ten minutes."

Before Rick manages to dress himself and put on a life jacket, the wind has already arrived which often means the rain is not far behind.

"Quick!"

He walks straight to the mast. The night is very dark; it is raining cats and dogs, so we cannot see or hear each other. But we've reefed the mainsail so many times that our movements are already automatic. There is no need to talk. We both do our part, and in ten seconds the sail is safely third reefed and we are hove-to.

Rick dries up and disappears back under the blanket. I am soaked too, but I stay outside to admire the surface of the sea boiling from the heavy rain. Knowing that the sails are properly squared away and that we are not in danger, I can fully enjoy watching the storm.

I have been watching the sea for more than thirty years. As far back as I can remember, the sea has always been there. I was born looking at the blue horizon and never took my eyes off it. Even when I did not actually see it, simply knowing it was somewhere close by gave me comfort. Comfort may be an understatement. Actually, it feels more like oxygen. To me, the sea represents the open side of my world. The escape route. New possibilities. Freedom.

When I was a baby, my mum would take me for walks around the bay in my hometown of Sistiana, Italy. Even at that early age, I could not seem to get enough of that sparkling water spreading toward infinity. When I grew up, I taught dinghy sailing in the local yacht club, so the sea became my office too. From early morning to late afternoon, I spent many summer days taking care of young sailors flying around in Optimist dinghies across Sistiana's glittering bay.

After work, there was a beer or two with the children's parents or long beach parties with friends. I cannot recall how many times I crashed in the hammock in the yacht club's courtyard. There was no point driving home for four hours sleep. Or maybe there was, and I just liked the idea of sleeping by the sea too much. So that's where I spent most of my summers, playing in the sunshine.

But to me, the sea was not only work and play. The sea was also where I sought shelter from the storms of my life, where I would look for answers or consolation. A walk by the sea was always my therapy.

I especially loved the sea in the winter. During the summer, the bay is full of tourists and local families, but in the winter storms, it was just me. I had my favorite bay all for myself! I was an addict, and, like most addicts, I never really understood the depth of my addiction until I had to give it up.

During my student years, I moved to Ljubljana to study at the university. Ljubljana is Slovenia's capital and is an amazing city, full of life, art, and opportunities. It was a big change from my little hometown where everyone knew everybody else and nothing exciting ever happened. I had a great time meeting new people every day (what a novelty that was!) and discovering everything that the student life had to offer. And yet every weekend I could barely wait to get back to the coast. It is about an hour's drive, and I remember clearly how the first faint tang of salt air would affect me as I neared the end of the journey. Before going home to see my family, I would always drive down to the sea, just to make sure it was still where I had left it.

After completing my studies, I got a teaching job in the pretty inland town of Otočec. The local school was on the edge of a forest, not far from the stunning river Krka. The children were wonderful and so were my colleagues. The school director was inspiring and gave me all the support and freedom that I needed to excel. Nevertheless, at the end of my first academic year, I had to leave. I walked into the director's office and reluctantly told her that, despite my love of the school and the people who staffed it, I could not stay. I told her in total honesty,

"I miss the sea too much."

A few weeks later I got a job on the coast in Izola, and, despite the more urban setting and enormous class sizes, I was as happy as a clam. My classroom had a wonderful view of the bay. I would watch sailing boats tacking and gybing whilst explaining photosynthesis to eager young minds.

I think that those born by the sea are somehow marked by it. We may not know it, but we simply cannot live without it.

In my bay, I have my own rock where I can sit and look toward the horizon. That's where I go in difficult moments, and I know the sea will comfort me.

When I am joyful, the sea is happy with me.

When I feel like shouting my lungs out, it calms me.

When I am running on empty, the sea fills me with energy again.

And it always gives me hope.

The sea has never failed to deliver the answer. Even if that answer is just a whisper reassuring me that tomorrow is going to be a better day.

Many years ago, I wrote a love poem on that very rock, titled "You Are My Sea."

I love you like

I love the sea.

I admire you both

from the distant shores.

I am standing right here.

I can touch you.

You feel so close

but I want more.

I look toward the horizon

I see you're far

I'll never make it.

But what is hiding there?

How will I get to you?

You are my stormy sea,

the danger hanging

over me.

Other times you are

a calm lagoon

where I can

take shelter.

But the horizon is calling.

What is there?

Why don't you let me sail to it?

You are my sea,

I love you both

without fear.

You are my sea,

I'll keep chasing

the horizon.

I wrote this poem for the prince of my angsty teenage years. At the time, I craved to get closer to him, to look over the horizon into his soul. But today I read these lines differently. I actually think that the horizon is not a metaphor at all. At the time, I did not realize that this poem contained a clue to my future. I will always be more excited by the actual horizon than the poetic one. My greatest love will always be the sea, and I will spend my life chasing it. I will have to go through storms and calms, but it really does not matter. When we love someone, we accept all his or her facets. Of course, we prefer when our companion is happy and in a good mood, but this does not mean that we stop loving him when he is sad or angry.

Anyway, I am increasingly convinced that I do not love the sea despite the difficult currents and the wild storms, but because of them. Just how dull would it be if the sea was dead calm and never scared or challenged us?

April 22, 2014: Color Me Blue

I am slowly being overwhelmed by the intense blueness of everything.

I am streaked by a precisely defined shade of blue which cannot be found anywhere else in the world.

I travel back to my school years and remember our art teacher who, at the beginning of the year, would list which paint colors we needed to buy. She was picky. We could not buy just any type of red (perish the thought!). She specifically asked for red cadmium. The same was true for all colors, particularly blues. She would not accept cobalt, cyan, or navy, but would demand ultramarine.

Looking back, I think that she may have been a sailor who has seen the real color of the deep ocean.

The sea has countless shades of blue, but ultramarine is what is all around us out here in mid-ocean. I do not know the proper terminology to describe colors (or wine, for that matter), so let me simply say that this color is overwhelming in its intensity. I cannot liken it to something else, because I have never seen a blue of such depth anywhere else in the world. It's the result of over two miles of clear ocean water. Depth is everything.

April 23, 2014: Admiration

Nothing special happened today. The only thing worth mentioning is that we'll soon be entering the southern hemisphere. The closer we get to the equator, the more often I check our position on the GPS. At the moment, our latitude is one degree and 56 minutes north, which means that we can expect to cross it tomorrow or the day after.

I am thinking about how we can read countless books, watch movies, and listen to stories about ocean sailing, but if we really want to know anything about it, we just have to go and do it ourselves. There is simply nothing that can replace the experience.

Rick knows this very well; he is most certainly a doer. He is an extraordinary captain; although ten years ago, he knew nothing about boats. One day he decided to learn to sail, and he simply bought a boat. He went through the RYA Yachtmaster course, but after that, it was all learning through experience.

Before that, he used to have an equestrian center in Spain. That was his first business of its kind, but with hard work and commitment, he managed to raise it to the top level to become one of the most highly regarded riding centers in Europe.

Prior to that, he used to lead overland safari trips throughout Africa. He has some incredible stories from that time. Some so unbelievable I would probably have taken them with a pinch of salt if I hadn't seen the photographs.

Those years in Africa gave him precious memories, but also a valuable experience in diesel mechanics (very helpful on a boat!) and the ability to manage a large group of people in demanding conditions.

Before all this, he used to earn his living as a tenor saxophonist. He was self-taught, but with intense practice, he managed to reach a professional level. He played with some good names on the London music scene, and in one particular two-year period somehow managed to perform an astonishing 600 gigs.

I know I am biased, but I really think that we could all learn some important lessons from his life story. What I most admire about him is his extraordinary curiosity and his belief that anyone can re-invent themselves at any time. The fact that this kind of re-invention means repeated intense learning curves has never deterred him. When he wanted to turn the page, he simply turned it.

April 24, 2014: Knowledge

The first part of the night is extremely calm. The wind is so light that the wind vane cannot steer. I am not very excited at the idea of standing at the helm, as we are barely moving, but when I let the boat steer herself, she chooses to turn back toward Mexico. That's just too much! There is still a very big psychological difference in facing the wrong direction - even when you are practically standing still. I eventually decide to lie down in the cockpit so I can watch the starry sky while having one hand on the helm. I pick a star and make sure that *Calypso* is always facing that direction. I love it when I follow the stars instead of the compass. I feel like an old sea dog.

While I enjoy the beauty of the night, two stars shoot across the sky. What should I ask for? The only request I send into the sky is a safe passage. I really do not need anything else.

The calm sea is rocking me like a baby in a cradle, and I occasionally doze off with my hand on the helm. My sporadic snoozing is interrupted for last time at four in the morning, when the wind fills in. I jump up excitedly. Could we have finally reached the trade winds that, supposedly, should push us all the way to the finish line? If so, life on board *Calypso* is about to get a whole lot easier. And if not easier, then at least faster.

The breaking of the day soon dampens my enthusiasm as the dawn does nothing to dispel the darkness which, it now seems, was more a product of the black clouds than the absence of the sun. At least I am beginning to understand them better. I have done nothing but stare at them for weeks now and have learned which ones are a threat and which ones are benign. I know that those coming from the north and from the west are not a danger to us. I also know that those without rain do not bring a significant change in the wind. I do not reef the sails at all if I do not see rain on the horizon. I know that large black clouds which stretch across a significant portion of the sky are not dangerous if there is light underneath them.

Ten days ago, I didn't know any of this.

Whilst watching five or six black clouds at different points on the horizon, some raindrops fall from the one directly above me. I do not even move the cockpit cushions or close the hatches because I know it is not going to last long. I step under the rain hoping for a morning shower but there is barely enough water for a bird to bathe in. Then I look west where a big rainbow is forming over the sea. It rises slowly, inch by inch, until it takes up the entire sky with a full half-circle. It is magnificent. My first rainbow on the ocean. I savor its intense colors in the morning light and choose to believe they are announcing a wonderful day.

Surprisingly, I am right. The clouds eventually dissipate, and the sun shines all morning, which is a real balm for our souls and for the batteries – both of which needed a little recharging. There is enough sunshine to turn on the fridge again while also charging the computer and the battery for my camera. I think again about how, out here, small things can make me so happy.

After my morning nap, I take over the watch and Rick goes below to sleep. As soon as I hear a light snore, I tiptoe to the forepeak where I have hidden a silver crown – part of a Neptune costume that I assembled in Mexico - so that we could properly perform the traditional ritual at the equator. I then spent the rest of the afternoon cutting old newspaper to make a wig and a beard to complete the outfit. The equator is only 38 miles away. After we cross it, there will only be an additional 960 miles to Hiva Oa. While it is generally stated (often by me) that it is better to travel than to arrive, I suspect that we have both started counting down the days.

April 25, 2014: Milestone

Tonight, for the first time in this voyage, I was hoping for no wind. At midnight, we were only twenty miles from the equator and, if we were to sail fast, we would reach this important milestone in the middle of the night. While there is nothing particularly wrong with this, it would be a shame to miss one of the rare landmarks on a featureless ocean, even one that only exists on paper and in the mind of navigators. Sailing into another hemisphere sounds like a great excuse to mark this day, and the whole ritual would be better served by daylight.

Crossing the equator is a great achievement for every sailor, and maritime tradition demands that it must be celebrated appropriately. There are strict protocols to follow as you make the rite of passage between "pollywog" (novice sailor) to "shellback" (old salt). Today we are still pollywogs. Tomorrow, when we cross the longest parallel for the first time, we will be old salty shellbacks and officially allowed to bore people in bars.

Neptune himself - the King of all the seas and oceans - must lead the ritual on board. Usually, the captain plays this part, and Rick, with his great rhetoric, is perfect for the job. He does not know that I have prepared a costume for him to enhance the performance, nor did he see me sneak a bottle of champagne into the fridge in preparation for the big ceremony. Everything is ready, but as I would like to capture this special celebration with my camera, I need daylight. So, for the first time, I am more than happy to be moving at the speed of a sleepy turtle.

At eight o'clock in the morning, the wind fills in and the equator approaches rapidly. I cannot contain my excitement, so I wake Rick up, stick a cup of tea under his nose, and show him his new outfit.

"Where did you get that?" he laughs. "I would never have thought of it."

I am not sure why he is so surprised. Isn't a King Neptune outfit a mandatory item on every ocean-going boat?

At 10.20 a.m., we finally cross the invisible line with the latitude of zero degrees, zero minutes and zero seconds. I was hoping to cross it at the 127th meridian, because 27 is Rick's lucky number, but the ocean current has different ideas. So I have to settle for a longitude slightly shy of that. The weather is splendid; the wind is just perfect; and we are in a very festive mood. We decide to save the champagne for the end of the trip in favor of toasting with Mexican beer. Rick takes his new role very seriously and speaks as a great sage. In Neptune's sermon, he thanks the ocean for keeping us safe during our navigations in the northern hemisphere and asks him to keep taking care of us in the southern seas.

To show our gratitude, we offer him a sip of Mexican beer and two gold coins. The first coin to fly into the ocean is a Mexican peso. I'm not sure if that's enough, so I also sacrifice the only Euro we have on the boat.

Somewhere I read that, if you throw a penny into the deepest ocean, it would take more than three hours to travel to the bottom. It is a scary yet magnificent thought. I am trying to imagine its journey. It must be so dark and quiet down there.

The equator is also the point that more or less marks the end of the doldrums - the area filled with squalls and calms that have been plaguing us for the last week or so. Hopefully, they are behind us now.

I remember how scared I was of crossing the doldrums, but the worries were actually worse than reality. In fact, we never had much more than 30 knots of wind.

Is that not always the case with fear? Isn't every academic exam much scarier in our nightmares than in reality? Isn't the hardest part of a job interview the evening before when we cannot calm our nerves enough to fall asleep? What about the lump in our throat that almost mutes us the moment we try to confess our feelings to our beloved? Do not most of our fears disappear as soon as we confront them?

Enough introspection for now because I just remembered that, before departing, I hid a bag of treats under the bed labeled "DO NOT OPEN UNTIL THE EQUATOR," and food is more fun than philosophy. This bag of goodies is nothing special, but today its contents will be more delicious than any restaurant fare. We haven't had such treats for a long time. I bought plenty, but they still ran out after the first week. Rick calls them fun food. I open the bag and pull out some prosciutto, rosemary crackers, cashew nuts, a big bag of dried fruit, and – best of all - chocolate covered blueberries.

April 26, 2014: Homesickness

Today is another beautiful sunny day. The sea is sparkling brightly in the afternoon sun, and the wind is just strong enough to form some whitecaps. The Italians have a nice name for these white peaks. They called them little geese. Perhaps they are. I can just imagine them - on surfboards, wearing Hawaiian shorts, and showing off to the other birds.

My daily vista is always the same, yet always beautiful. I never get tired of gazing at the horizon or staring at the water as it foams past the hull. The colors and sounds of the sea inspire me to scribble the deep life thoughts of that moment in my diary. Staring at the sea can be a better rest than sleep. The brain synchs to the rhythm and the body synchs to the brain.

I wonder if, after a month of wave-induced meditation, I will be able to reconnect to our crazy world of fast food and overstimulation. That is, of course, if the whole world has not blown itself to pieces while we have been away. Our civilization could have ended, and we wouldn't know a thing about it out here until we made landfall and noticed a slight reduction in bureaucracy.

We have not had access to any news during the voyage (we probably could find some on the radio but do not even try), and I find that this is actually a good thing.

For us, the mighty 21st century people, it is normal to be permanently reachable and to check our email at least once a day. On the sea it is different. Ocean sailing means a total disconnection from everything.

This vagabond lifestyle has also left me a little disconnected from old friends. I am far from up-to-date with what is going on back home. Sometimes one particular friend or another tries gamely to keep me in the loop by letting me know that "Lara just had another baby" when I didn't even know about the first one, or that couples who I had no idea were together have just split up. Over time, I have accepted the fact that I just cannot be up-to-date with everything, although I really appreciate it when my closest friends send me a monthly summary. At least I can follow their lives a little better.

From their reports, I see the world going on without me. Relatives and friends graduate, get married, move house, have kids, and die, but I am never there to see it. Sometimes it hurts me not being there with them and for them. If I were rich, this would probably be the only thing that I would change in my life: I would fly home more often.

At the same time, these long absences have taught me how to recognize a true friend. On the rare occasions that I go home and reconnect with everybody, it is usually much easier than I might have imagined. The time that has separated us like a big soap bubble is easily burst by the first hug. Nothing has been permanently broken and we can continue our friendship as if I had merely been to Greece for a week's holiday. But this miracle does not happen with everyone. This is another insight I owe to traveling.

April 27, 2014: Terror

I am very tired. We have strong winds; the sea is boisterous; and the big waves are slamming into *Calypso*. Just as I thought I was over it, I am seasick again – although probably more due to fatigue than the motion of the boat. I cannot watch movies or read books. Nothing. I am sitting at the navigation table, staring at the GPS screen in front of me, looking at the slowly-passing numbers, monitoring our course and speed.

I am staring at them and hoping to get through the night.

I stare for an hour.

Two.

Three.

Four.

This is the longest watch I have ever done.

The clock has never moved so slowly.

The only good thing is that the strong breeze turns the wind turbine quickly, generating plenty of power, and I can therefore have the radar on permanently. I still go outside regularly, but with this sickness, it really takes all of my willpower to climb up those three rolling stairs every twenty minutes.

When I finally go off watch, one of the lines of the wind vane breaks. Rick jumps to the helm and steers manually. A minute later, the next big wave approaches us from behind, crashes into the boat, and the helm turns freely. Suddenly we have no control over the boat. Both auto-steering systems have given up, and now the wheel has followed them into redundancy! We look at each other in shock, and Rick says what we are both thinking:

"If the cable is broken, that's no big deal. But if there is something wrong with the rudder, this trip will not end well."

The only thing we have left is the emergency tiller, which we keep handy for such emergencies. I insert it into its hole and, thank goodness, I am steering again which means that the rudder is still attached to the boat. The problem is that the tiller is quite short and, in such a lively seaway, quite difficult to operate. When a gust comes, I have to hang on like a koala to its mamma.

I hand steer while Rick hauls all the gear out of the cockpit locker and burrows into the cramped steering compartment. Fortunately, he soon discovers that the steering cables have broken. Very fixable if you have a spare which, of course, we do. Thank Neptune! Odd though. We replaced them before leaving Mexico. A brand-new quarter-inch steel cable has literally disintegrated!

We cannot repair it just yet because the sea is too rough. Rick thinks that it might be easier to replace the broken wind vane line, which means that the self-steering could take over the task. We have a type of self-steering that connects directly to the rudder quadrant (rather than via the wheel), so it would work independently of the broken steering cables. We shorten the sails to slow us down and moderate the motion of the boat while Rick once again plunges head first into the steerage compartment. (I am beginning to think he likes it in there). In about half an hour, he manages to fix the self-steering which is very good news as it is now the only thing that stands between us and a thousand miles of hand steering with a tiny emergency tiller which was clearly designed to work in flat conditions only. The electric autopilot (after its brief rise from the dead) has started acting up again, and the wheel is now useless until the new cable is fitted.

For lunch we heat up one of the pre-made Indian dishes I bought, a delicious butter chicken. It is very tasty, but we are not enjoying the food; our thoughts are somewhere else. After lunch, I finally lie down, and two hours later I send Rick to a forced rest.

Just before sunset, a little squall arrives, this time more powerful than usual. I am barely able to furl in the genoa.

I feel that I am running out of puff.

I am so looking forward to landfall.

During the squall, I see a colorful buoy fly past. We missed it by about two feet. I stare at the red dot, which is rapidly disappearing in our wake, with an open mouth. Do you know what the chances are of hitting something in the middle of the Pacific Ocean? It is like throwing an orange in the air blindfolded and hoping to hit a bird.

On the evening radio net, I report our trouble with the steering. It is always prudent to inform the fleet of any problems, however minor. If something goes wrong, the rescuers can have a better guess at our situation.

The night is anything but friendly. The sea has grown, and I am, I admit it, terrified. The worst is when I hear the threatening foam approaching. Once again I wonder if this wave will pass under the boat, smash into her, or fill the cockpit with water. Rick cannot sleep. He is concerned by every little noise and creak that the boat makes as she wracks and turns over the large seas. Finally, he tells me what is troubling him most:

"I really hate the fact that the boat is not a hundred percent at the moment. I wish the weather was calmer so we could stop her and repair everything that needs to be done."

We reef the sails, slow the boat, bear off the wind - nothing helps. Finally, I convince him to dive into a book. When he finally falls asleep, I look at the clock: it is five in the morning. Soon it will be dawn, but I will not wake him up, he really needs to rest.

During my watch, I hear something banging in the steering compartment. It worries me, but I really do not want to wake him up now, just as he finally managed to fall asleep. I could try to empty the cockpit locker and climb in myself, but I look for excuses not to do it.

The boxes are just too heavy for me to lift out of the locker.

It is a two-person job.

It is dark.

It is rough.

I would soon feel seasick.

I probably couldn't fix it anyway.

I hope and pray that nothing is wrong, and I promise that we will check the situation when the day breaks. It worries me because with no autopilot and steering wheel, the wind vane is on its own. It cannot give up. No way.

The good news is that it is only 600 miles to landfall.

I am predicting a nervy week.

April 28, 2014: Joy

The wind has eased up slightly so our progress is slower, but we still have a strong current that is pushing us reliably toward the Marquesas. I let Rick sleep until 9 a.m., which seemed only fair as I intend to shove him straight back into the hole to investigate the troubling noises. Fortunately, they turn out to be nothing, so the black thoughts of last night have departed. I hope for some pleasant sailing.

When I go to bed, I toss and turn for a while. I am exhausted but cannot shut my eyes. I think I may still be full of adrenaline from yesterday. I watch a movie, eat some leftovers from last night's dinner, and when I finally fall asleep, it is already one o'clock. Rick spends the afternoon dancing on the boomkin to some lively music. Now that *Calypso* is fixed, he is smiling again, full of positivity.

Even though there is less wind, the waves have not abated. I still need to hold on with one hand whilst cooking with the other. Breaking my own rule for just one second, I reach for a spice on the high shelf. I am immediately airborne, flying to the other side of the cabin. Ouch, another bruise on my bum.

Later I take on a few small jobs. I check the fridge (which has been emitting a strange smell for two days) and I find a forgotten pear. I double bag the rubbish and put it under the sink. We have room for six bags there; so far we've filled four. I prepare a few bottles of cordial with water. I clean the stove while thinking about how little we fight.

Rick is trying to convince me to dance on the boomkin:

"It really is the best gym."

He has been trying to sell that idea for a while, but until now I was too lazy to listen. Today I have more energy, so I put the headphones on and hit the boomkin, which provides a little dance floor surrounded by stainless steel and aluminum that will stop me falling overboard. Aquatic cage dancing, if you will. It is also far enough from the cabin that I can sing without waking Rick up. I turn on the music; I wiggle my bum a few times, and I realize that Rick was right. This is so much fun!

As the music begins to work its magic, I begin to really enjoy myself. I stomp, jump, wiggle, and sing at the top of my voice. The blood pumps strongly in my veins and the extra oxygen seems to bring the fun all the way to the tips of my fingers and toes.

I feel amazing.

I feel immensely free.

The endless ocean flies by me; the wind is filling the sails. The sun warms my skin, and I do not miss anything.

At this moment, I am a little dot in the middle of the vast ocean. Nobody sees me; no one can hear me. I can scream and jump as much as I wish. My heart is bursting with happiness and my eyes fill up with tears.

If a plane had flown past, the pilot would have seen what appeared to be a small floating shell with an obviously mad, naked woman gyrating crazily and cackling at the top of her voice. He would also have seen an insanely happy person.

April 29, 2014: Senses

Today I like the sea again. I am trying to breath it, to fill my lungs with its vastness. I would like to bottle this moment of complete freedom and save it as the most precious treasure. I know that someday I will miss these days. The ocean is under my skin and in each of my senses.

For a month, I have listened to the noise of water - day and night - regardless of what else I was doing. Whether I was reading, cooking, writing, or sleeping, the sound of the water hissing by the hull has been a permanent soundtrack. My eyes have become so accustomed to the overwhelming blueness of the sky and sea that I am unsure if they will be able to cope with the gray of tarmac or the green of meadows.

I constantly smell the sea too. We all know how good for the soul and the body the ocean air is. This is partly why I was never worried about our health on this long journey. Since I have been living on the sea, I have yet to get sick once.

The search for balance has gradually become automatic. My whole body has become accustomed to the waves and the need to synchronize every action with the movement of the boat. Every single task, however small (opening a door, raising a glass, biting an apple, sitting down, putting on glasses), must be done between one wave and the next. After the first three days of sailing, the rolling became so normal that I didn't even think about it anymore. I actually noticed that I could predict what the boat was doing even while sitting down below. If the boat leaned differently or changed its angle to the waves, I immediately knew that something was wrong and went outside to check it out. One gains an automatic appreciation of what type of movement is acceptable, and anything that falls outside that range gets the internal warning lights flashing.

April 30, 2014: Sunrise

Oh, how I enjoy it when the boat flies!

I keep repeating to myself and others that speed is not important, but I would be lying if I didn't admit that I prefer sailing fast. When the sails are full of wind and the boat is nicely inclined and streams through the water like a rocket - this is a truly satisfying feeling. We are clocking up very decent 120-mile days at the moment; our best run being yesterday when we managed to set a new record of 143 miles. Not bad for a traditional old cutter with only 30 feet at the waterline. If we had managed this kind of speed for the whole journey, we would already be drinking coconut rum in the Marquesas!

In Mexico, I estimated the journey would take thirty days. However, we have encountered more calms than expected, so it will take slightly longer. Somewhere in the middle of the trip, we made a bet about when we would reach Polynesia. Rick chose May 10th while I picked the 4th. It is the last day of April and Hiva Oa is a mere 300 miles away, so it looks as if I am going to win (not sure what though).

I am noticing that the more we approach the end of the journey, the more I enjoy being out here. With every mile, the worries decrease as the proximity of land brings a sense of security and an opportunity to make repairs. If something happens here, someone may even come out to help or bring a part. In the middle of the ocean, we knew very well that we were on our own. On the high seas, the smallest problem can have very serious repercussions.

We have very steady trade winds and a strong ocean current helping us, so we now feel we'll get there one way or another, even dismasted.

In a few days, this great adventure will come to an end, and our lives will go back to usual. We'll sleep at night and spend the days together. It sounds great and I am looking forward to it, but I must also admit that I am slightly sorry to lose our newfound rhythm of sleep, eat, watch the ocean, sleep, eat, watch the ocean. I have become so accustomed to this routine that every other way of spending my days now seems a little unnatural. I am especially fond of the night watches. Every day I watch the night giving way to the day, and I love every variety of it. One day the sunrise is a fiery red, the next day a blend of pastel colors. Another time it is so cloudy that I cannot even see the rising sun. In these moments, I realize how many beautiful scenes I must have missed in my previous life on land. As a student, I would enter the university building early in the morning when it was still dark and step out after a full day of lectures, back into the dark again. How many wonderful sunrises and sunsets did I miss?

My favorite university teacher was our professor of physics. He wanted to prove how much fun physics could be and always gave us the most interesting homework. One of these was to watch the sunset. That's right, he wanted us to watch the sunset from exactly the same place for a month. We had to draw the horizon (for example, the outline of hills or houses) on a transparent plastic foil to be sure we always had the same point of view. Every evening we had to position the foil in front of us, match it with the real horizon, and mark with a red dot the exact spot where the sun disappeared. What we 'discovered' is old news indeed: the fact that the sun sets in a different place every day. The goal of the assignment was to introduce youngsters to astronomy, but it also gave us something else. For the first time in my life, I took the time to watch all the phases of the sunset every day for a month.

My observation site was in my home bay and when I realized the wonderful performances that were going on every day in front of my eyes, I began to carry a camera with me. I still keep all those wonderful photos. It really is a shame that too often we do not take the time to admire what is happening around us.

On the boat, it is a very different story altogether. Here, time is the only thing I have in abundance. I like sitting in the cockpit when the night slides away and makes room for a new morning. I love to follow all the stages of it. First the stars disappear. Then the sky becomes less black, and shapes slowly begin to appear. Gradually I see more and more details. Finally, it is light enough that I can turn off my head torch, although the sun is not up yet. Then, somewhere on the horizon a glowing ball starts to appear, and the sky puts on a fiery costume. Sometimes I whisper:

"Welcome, new day."

May 1, 2014: Challenges

The state of our fresh provisions is telling me (as if I needed to be told) that we are almost at the Marquesas. At lunch, I used the last two zucchini, and now we only have a dozen lemons, three apples, some onions, and a few potatoes left. I am quite pleased with myself for buying pretty much the right amount of fruit and veggies. Even those ninety eggs didn't go off, thanks to my diligent care. Now we have twenty-four left and I suspect they will not be good much longer, so I am making a big pile of pancakes every morning. We are certainly not starving, but I admit that I started to dream about fruit salads and crunchy green lettuces.

Today I am nervous for a different reason. In an unguarded moment of helpfulness, I volunteered to be tonight's net controller. Most volunteer controllers set out from the Americas well before us and have now completed the crossing, creating a need for a controller to record the positions of the ten or so boats that are still out here. I have been avoiding it all month in the belief that my English is not good enough. Actually, I know that I do not make too many mistakes. Most Europeans have no big problems with my foreign accent (a mix of Slovenian and Italian that some people have mistaken for French), but when I speak to Americans on the radio, we often just do not understand each other. Nevertheless, Rick convinced me to take up the challenge, so tonight I will lead the Pacific Puddle Jump Net on the SSB radio.

This radio is a complex toy, and you need a license to use it. When I first looked at the exam questions, I just shook my head. I knew straight away that I would never understand what this is all about. But at the same time, I needed the license. I didn't have much choice but to try and find a way. I am a teacher after all, so if there is something I know, it is how to pass exams. With various mnemonics and other tricks, I managed to memorize all the 358 right answers and surprise the commission with a 100% result.

"Amazing result, lady," drawled the American examiner. "You really know your stuff. You should try to do the next level as well! Its free, you cannot lose anything by trying!"

"Hmmm... maybe another time." I sheepishly replied, knowing that a score of 0% would reveal my total lack of understanding of the subject. I suddenly had to run somewhere to a very important meeting.

In the last three years, I have used the radio almost every day, but I still have absolutely no idea how it works. I couldn't tell a Henri from a Farad if my life depended on it. All the terminology that other radio operators use is pretty much Greek to me (or possibly "geek"). Some even talk in numbers! The number 73, for example, is a greeting.

Sometimes I have the paranoid suspicion that these voices may be coming from space. Perhaps this is the Martian way of taking over the planet.

"This is Romeo Sierra Mike with traffic for Bravo Lima Tango. Over."

I always hope they will not uncover me and start pointing, like in the finale of *Invasion of the Body Snatchers*.

To be able to communicate via SSB, one has to learn some basic terms and, of course, the International Alphabet. I use it most often to spell my name, which for some reason seems impossibly complicated to English-speaking people. On the sea, my name is spelled: Juliet Alfa Sierra November Alfa. My captain is Romeo India Charlie Kilo. In Australia, we met a couple who named their boat with the International Alphabet version of their initials. If we were to do this, our boat would be called *Romeo Juliet* and would make everybody sick.

It is eight o'clock. Time for the net, so I gather my courage and click the transmit button.

"Is this frequency in use?"

There is no answer, so I can begin:

"Welcome to the Pacific Puddle Jump net for today, May 1st, 2014. Today's net is run by *Calypso*, Kilo Delta Zero Romeo Sierra Mike. Our current position is 7 degrees 53 minutes south, 136 degrees 14 minutes west. We have 12 knots of wind from the east-south-east, a 20% cloud cover and the barometer shows 1008 mb. Our course over ground is 206 degrees magnetic, and we are currently sailing under full sails at five knots."

Next comes a question, which is the same in all radio nets around the world:

"Before we open the net, is there any emergency, medical, or priority traffic?"

If nobody is having any problems, we can proceed to the task of recording all the positions and progress reports from our fellow sea gypsies as they deal with precisely the same challenges we face.

Only seven boats check in today. Except for the ketch *Rhapsody*, which is two days behind us, all the others are very far away. Some have just left Mexico, while others have already arrived in the Marquesas.

I have a short chat with all the boats, but they have very little to report. I soon close the net with the standard message:

"This concludes today's net. We had six boats underway and one at anchor. Tomorrow's net will be run by SV *Green Panther*. This is *Calypso*, Kilo Delta Zero Romeo Sierra Mike. The Pacific Puddle Jump net is now closed, and this frequency is now clear."

Rick congratulates me while I wipe the sweat from my forehead:

"You did well!"

Actually, it was not as bad as I expected. And we're back to that familiar point about fear again! All expectations are worse than reality. Perhaps this is the lesson I will take from this ocean passage. Is it really that simple?

May 2, 2014: Values

Landlubbers often ask me why I like life at sea. There are many answers. I certainly love the simplicity and freedom that it brings, but the people I meet also play an important role. They are my sailing tribe, the sea gypsies.

In our tribe, no one ever asks you which school you attended or whether you even went to school. Nobody is interested in how much money you have in the bank, how you dress, or if you are badly groomed. Nobody cares if you have a shiny, expensive boat (much to the annoyance of shiny, expensive boat owners). There is no status in the sailing tribe other than your ability to tie a rolling hitch in a gale or splice an eye into an anchor rode. This tribe has more respect for the things that really matter, like...

* being kind to others

* being a good host

* being ready to help whenever and wherever (whether or not it will take you all day, whether you need to change your plans, and whether you may damage your property or put yourself in trouble)

* having handy skills

* being good company

* being able to adjust

* respecting the environment.

Nobody is interested in whether you have a PhD in neuroscience or if you are a millionaire. If you can fix an engine, splice double braid, or bake a good loaf of bread, you will do.

In our tribe, there are many unusual people whom the land has rejected and who have rejected land. Nobody condemns them here. Nobody cares if they walk around barefoot or have a tattoo on their face.

I often remember a friend from Australia who once mentioned to me that he only has three t-shirts. I was so proud of myself for having known him for two years and not even noticing it.

Image has become so important in modern society that whoever neglects it is considered weird. I have always struggled to find the motivation to dress myself nicely, take care of my wild hair, or put on makeup. Even when I lived in the civilized world, I went to the hairdresser every two years, and I have always worn my shoes until they fell apart. My sister often laughs at the peculiar collection of footwear under my bed: mountaineering boots, jazz dance shoes, neoprene windsurf boots, climbing shoes, snowboard boots, and fins.

I am almost forty, and I still have no idea how to match clothes, apply makeup, or dress properly. And quite frankly, I really don't give a damn. The money I "should" spend on fashionable accessories, jewelry, handbags, shoes, and the like, I would much rather invest in a windsurfer or a monofin so I can pretend to be a mermaid. I buy most of my clothes second-hand and choose them purely on serviceability. The only thing I buy new are bikinis, which

Rick picks out based on what he calls his "internal sauciness scale."

For many years I thought that something was wrong with me, until I moved to the sea where I found my tribe. At sea, we are all a little odd in appearance and quite proud to be so.

Today is another very slow day. We silently dream of seeing land tomorrow, but it does not matter anymore. Now that we are so close, we are no longer in a hurry. We know that we have succeeded.

The boat is limping, but that was to be expected. Rick suggests that we make a list of all the breakages.

1.   The most worrying failure is the water ingress through the bobstay chain plate on the bow. The flow of water was fairly constant, but today it is minimal because the sea has flattened considerably. So, probably nothing serious, but it will have to come off for inspection.

2.   The autopilot has failed. This will be the most expensive repair, if it can be repaired at all. As with all over-complicated things you bring on board, replacement is probably the inevitable answer.

3.   A steering cable broke, so we cannot use the wheel and will have to anchor using the emergency tiller instead. No big deal, as we have a spare cable which will be easy to fit when the boat stops rolling.

4.   The genoa is torn on the bottom edge. This will be my next sewing project.

5.   The complicated system to extend the spinnaker pole has failed. So, for the last week, we could use only half of the genoa and were therefore much slower. This will be Rick's project, and I suspect it not to be a simple one.

6.   The new Parasailor has more than twenty new holes, but I have already patched them on the way.

7.   The mainsail got a small rip. I already repaired it this morning. (I discovered that it is much easier to sew while sailing because the sail itself is nicely stretched and tight.)

In short, a lot of small failures, but fortunately nothing really serious. So, I can state categorically that *Calypso* has performed really well. Looking back, I do not regret that we spent so much time preparing her for the ocean, as this gave us a great passage and extra confidence in bad weather. We were personally well prepared too - as sailors, as a team, and as a couple. We knew it would be demanding, and we did everything we could to reduce the likelihood of accidents. Maybe I could say that it wasn't as demanding as I expected it might be. But it certainly wasn't easy. We faced a number of challenges and, if we had not been ready for them, the outcome may have been different. Maybe I could congratulate myself, Rick, and *Calypso*, but I am not going to do it. Tomorrow is another day and we still have plenty of time to mess it up.

May 3, 2014: Impermanence

Today is Rick's birthday! I do not believe in cake-free birthdays, so I did some baking during the last hour of the watch. I tiptoed around trying not to wake him and ruin the surprise. When the cake went into the oven, I pulled out a bottle of champagne and placed it in the fridge.

Then I took out the French, British, and Slovenian flags and run them up the mast with the yellow square which signals we are in quarantine. *Calypso* is now ceremonially dressed to enter a new country.

After half an hour, I checked on the cake. What a disaster! The full kettle on the stove top tilted the oven and the result is a cake that is two inches tall on one side and half an inch tall on the other. Half the cake is still raw, and the other half is as black as *Calypso's* bottom. Total fail, but I do not give up. The failed cake gets reinvented as a sweet Frisbee and flies to the sharks while I set about re-making the dough. This time, I remove the kettle from the stove top and make sure the oven can move freely to stay more or less horizontal.

I am happy to report that it worked! (The cake was still slightly tilted, but only slightly).

The unusual smell of baked chocolate cake wakes Rick up. I add some good news to make his morning even better:

"Only seventy miles to go!"

So, if the wind picks up just a little bit, we will see land today. Although at the moment, we're moving slower than a snail again. Clearly, King Neptune does not care as much about Rick's birthday as I do.

Oh gosh, I cannot wait to step back on land! I have sooo had enough of being on the boat for now. I want to jump, sprint, twirl, and spin. I want to run myself ragged. All the cells of my body are asking me to get them off the boat. I am like a nervous horse in a starting gate.

I am constantly looking toward the horizon, although I know that I am not close enough to see anything yet. I am so impatient, I cannot sleep. Lying in bed staring at the ceiling, I think about life on the sea, about how authentic it is. There is no room for lying or pretending, and you cannot escape the strongest emotions.

At sea, there are moments of total despair and complete horror, of deep fulfillment and utter indifference. They come and fill you up, and you cannot resist them or pretend they are not there. On the ocean, all emotions are as intense and fleeting as the equatorial squalls.

There were times, in these past weeks, when I thought we might die. There were even times during bouts of seasickness when I wished I could die just to get away from it all.

The terror is deeper at sea than on land, but so is the joy. In the middle of the ocean, I never smiled out of courtesy, but I did laugh loudly, jump joyfully, and dance like a mad woman because I felt like it.

At sea, we learn that nothing lasts forever. Everything passes.

In some storms, we make the promise to never set foot on a boat again if we only survive. But when the storm passes and the sun returns, all those bad thoughts are immediately forgotten. In just one second, we are happy again. At the end of a hard sail, there is always a beautiful bay, and when we reach it, only satisfaction remains. Just like a sweaty climber at the top of a mountain looking at the view, thinking that it was well worth the effort. This is a completely different perspective than the one experienced by the person standing next to him who took the helicopter to the top and is wondering what all the fuss is about. The more demanding the climb, the more beautiful the view. This is also why the most beautiful moments at sea are the mornings after a storm.

May 4, 2014: Pride

I am so nervous, I keep moving from one end of the cockpit to the other without finding peace. I feel like a puppy that heard the master's car parking in the driveway. There is no way I could pick up a book or watch a movie. I need to be here, keeping my eyes sharp, sniffing the air. I feel the land getting closer, and I want to embrace this moment with all my senses when it deigns to arrive. It is a very dark night, so I cannot see the island, but man, can I sense it! I hope the dawn comes soon, or I may just explode with anticipation.

This feeling is probably the only thing I share with the early explorers of the oceans. Seeing land after weeks at sea is just as unforgettable today as it was hundreds of years ago. All sailors are impatient to see a little dot on the horizon.

But I was wrong again. The dawn begins to break and no little dot for me!

When the light starts unveiling more definite shapes, I can see a big black cloud off our starboard bow.

"I hope it will not bring any rain," I think to myself.

Just seconds later I realize my mistake: It is not a cloud; it is a bloody huge island! I was expecting a little far-away dot, not a huge mountain hovering over me. I must have under-estimated how tall this island is (and therefore from how far away it can be sighted).

I cannot believe it. We are here!

Rick is still asleep, but this time I just have to wake him up.

"LAND AHOY!"

He immediately comes out; we jump, dance, swear, and laugh like idiots. Yaaaaaaayy!!!

I cannot stop smiling as the clouds part and treat us to a glimpse of the lush tropical greenery of the island of Hiva Oa, replete with a rainbow. In a large arc, it descends from the clouds to the bay where we are heading. At the end of the rainbow, there is a safe, calm anchorage more valuable than any pot of gold.

The captain steers *Calypso* straight toward our goal while I go to the bowsprit and stare at the land, overwhelmed by the view of waves crashing into black rocks, tall green peaks, and the rainbow showing us the way.

Before this crossing, someone said to me, "You'll see. At the end, you'll not want it to be over."

For a whole month I thought, "What nonsense!" Today, for the first time, I understand those words.

The ocean somehow manages to trick us into a subtle addiction. It lures us into a gentle dependency that we wish to both leave and prolong simultaneously. Yet there is nothing really to be addicted to as there is nothing really out there. Perhaps the open ocean is addictive precisely for what it does not have. In an age when we all have too much, having less can become a real treasure. Less noise, less technology, less plastic, and less errands. Less confusion.

At 11 a.m. Mexican time and 9.30 a.m. Polynesian time, we anchor in Tahauku Bay on the island of Hiva Oa. After 32 days of sailing and over 3,000 nautical miles, we are finally in French Polynesia.

The tiny anchorage is full to the brim, so we must set two anchors, one off the bow and one off the stern so we don't swing and wipe out another boat. There is just not enough room for swinging to our anchor.

I expected a standing ovation or a solemn reception, but nobody even looks at us. Our sleepy neighbors are lost in thoughts over breakfast. A bearded young man is calmly rowing toward the shore. Some local fishermen pass by in a dug-out canoe, and a French sailor is casually pruning his toenails on the foredeck of his salt-encrusted aluminum sloop.

So what! We'll do it ourselves.

Rick and I don garlands and pop the champagne, which he delivers like a racing driver. We are quickly soaked in the sticky mess. We drink, congratulate one another, laugh, pour, kiss, and take photographs.

The plan was to rest, but suddenly we are not tired at all. We are just too euphoric, so we launch the dinghy and row ashore. I wonder if I can still walk on solid ground?

On the dock, we meet some crews we know from the radio net. Despite speaking every night for a month, this is the first time we have met. It is nice to put faces to the voices. Everybody congratulates us. We exchange stories and experiences from the ocean. I would normally gladly chat, but today I am in a hurry.

I politely say goodbye and pull Rick away. We look at each other, hold hands, and start running. Our legs do not want to stop. We run along the dirt road, among the fragrant flowering hibiscuses, frangipani, and coconut palm trees. The fresh air of this lush new country brings us new energy and we just keep running...

Epilogue

French Polynesia instantly enchanted us. After three years of the Mexican desert, the lush greenery of these islands is a welcome change. Sparkling green peaks proudly rise to the sky almost as if they are deliberately trying to find the earliest opportunity to show themselves to the tired sailors coming from the other end of the Pacific Ocean.

The village road is surrounded by beautiful tidy gardens colored by flowery bushes and fruit trees. On the road, we meet goats, horses, pigs, and an incredible amount of wild chickens. The locals are very friendly and like to offer a grapefruit or a mango from their garden to passing strangers. Drivers stop to offer a ride, regardless of whether we are hitchhiking. We are bombarded by the sweet scents of frangipani, mangoes, tiare, and bananas. Hiva Oa is actually just one big orchard. To sailors who have been dreaming of fresh food, it is a true paradise on earth.

In the evening, I sit in the cockpit and watch the high green peaks above me. Their tops are hidden in clouds, as usual. I breathe in fresh Polynesian air and think about the journey that is now behind us. Was it really so tough?

Actually, no. We were prepared for worse. I expected heavy sailing, mostly from a physical point of view. I thought that I would be tired, seasick, and feeling the lack of sleep. Of course, I was also worried about storms, big waves, strong winds, and lightning.

But it wasn't so bad. My body adjusted very quickly to both waves and our watch routine. We did not have any problems with exhaustion, thanks to our choice of long watches. With six hours of uninterrupted sleep, we always had a good, deep rest.

The weather spared us the worst. Only the doldrums were wider than expected. I was hoping for a 200-mile-wide belt of squalls and calms, but we got almost 500 miles of it.

The worst thing was something I had not predicted. I didn't know that when the land disappeared behind us, I would start wondering if the boat was really as indestructible as I had thought.

We had been preparing *Calypso* for this challenge for a long time, and I admit sometimes I thought we were over-doing it. When Rick suggested some new work or repair, I would think, "No need for it, everything is gonna be fine!"

I was convinced that we were already well prepared and that there was no reason for further delaying our departure. I was looking at others who were departing with much less preparation than us.

"If they can do it, so can we," I often said.

But when the distance from land increased, my belief that everything would be okay started to crumble. Over the last few weeks, I have discovered that no boat can be too prepared. I am very grateful to Rick, who insisted on much maintenance work that, at the time, I considered superfluous. Yes, constant worry is certainly the hardest part of this journey, and setting off unprepared will only exacerbate that.

But all this is now behind us, and we are left with pride and nice memories. Those less-nice memories will soon be dry-cleaned or forgotten. It is often said that a short memory is the reason that sailors go back to the sea and that women have more than one child.

I wonder if this trip has changed me.

Of course it has. Every trip does. But in what way?

After this voyage, I respect the power of nature even more. For some reason, I thought that, after crossing the ocean, I would think of myself as a better sailor, but the exact opposite has occurred. The ocean reminded me how much I still have to learn. This month has also taught me the true meaning of vastness and unveiled a new dimension of solitude. I discovered fears I did not know, and (last, but no less exciting) I lost two kilos!

My little world in the middle of the endless Pacific Ocean was very intimate and intense. It taught me a lot, but I sense that the lesson is not over yet.

I have that same feeling you get at the end of a really good movie on the big screen. Although the lights have come on, you cannot get up. You keep staring at the big white screen whilst waiting for everything that the director awakened in you to settle down.

That's why I am sitting here tonight, under this breathtaking Polynesian sky, carefully listening to nothing.

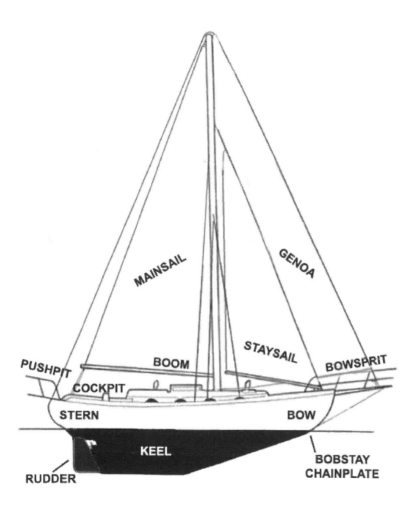

Calypso is a Union Polaris 36, a lovely double-ender based on a Robert Perry design. She is 36 ft (11 m) long.

Her length overall (including the pushpit and the bowsprit) is 44 feet (13 m). *Calypso* is a cutter and has a traditional long keel with an attached rudder. She was constructed in 1984 from fiberglass and old growth teak by the highly regarded Union shipyard in Taiwan. The interior joinery is beautifully crafted from teak and holly. *Calypso* weights 10 tons and her draft is 1.8 m.

We have seven sails: a mainsail with three reefs, a spare mainsail with three reefs, a staysail, a yankee, a large 150% genoa, a lightweight drifter and a Parasailor (a type of spinnaker with a wing to help it stay inflated). Both foresails have a rugged Spintec furling system.

Calypso is equipped with a 50 hp diesel engine (Perkins4-108), which we use as little as possible. Nevertheless, it is nice to know it is there if we need it.

Our electrical needs are met by six batteries, which we keep topped up with six solar panels and a wind generator.

We have a 540 liter water tank plus another 120 liters of drinking water in jerry cans. We consume approximately 8 liters of water a day, which means that we have about 80 days of autonomy. We top up our water supply with a cheap and simple rain catching system which can often extend our autonomy indefinitely.

We have 190 liters of diesel in the tanks and 80 liters in jerry cans, which is usually sufficient for several months. For our Pacific crossing we used 27 liters of fuel.

For communication we have a Standard Horizon VHF radio and an Icom 710 HF (SSB) radio. We also have a Pactor modem for sending e-mails via the HF radio.

A Furuno radar makes our life easier during the night.

The galley has a three-burner stove and a small oven which run on propane. When it gets too hot, we prefer to use the BBQ on the stern rail.

Our favorite piece of gear is the Cape Horn wind vane self-steering. We could not imagine crossing an ocean without it.

Thanks!

Thank you for coming along on this adventure. I hope you enjoyed it as much as I did, with all its highs and lows. If so, please take a moment to post a review.

If you have any questions, need some advice or would like to share some thoughts, please get in touch with me on my website www.jasnatuta.com.

I would be honoured to hear from you.

Fair winds and following seas!

Jasna Tuta

October 2018

Somewhere in Fiji

Printed in Great Britain
by Amazon

86061983R00100